A HANDBOOK OF PRICE THEORY

PRINCIPLES OF ECONOMICS SERIES

under the editorship of

EDWARD AMES

INTRODUCTION TO MACROECONOMIC THEORY
Edward Ames, State University of New York at Stony Brook

INDUSTRIAL ORGANIZATION: AN EMPIRICAL APPROACH
Stanley E. Boyle, Virginia Polytechnic Institute and State University

MACROECONOMIC ADJUSTMENTS
John A. Carlson, Purdue University

PRODUCTION AND TRADE
Peter W. Frevert, The University of Kansas

A HANDBOOK OF PRICE THEORY
Joseph P. McKenna, University of Missouri—St. Louis

NATIONAL INCOME AND OTHER SOCIAL ACCOUNTS
Sam Rosen, University of New Hampshire

INTRODUCTION TO INPUT-OUTPUT ECONOMICS
Chiou-shuang Yan, Drexel Institute of Technology

A HANDBOOK OF PRICE THEORY

JOSEPH P. McKENNA

UNIVERSITY OF MISSOURI—ST. LOUIS

Holt, Rinehart and Winston, Inc.

NEW YORK CHICAGO SAN FRANCISCO ATLANTA

DALLAS MONTREAL TORONTO LONDON SYDNEY

Library of Congress Catalog Card Number: 70-170202
ISBN: 0-03-078650-9
Printed in the United States of America
2 3 4 5 090 9 8 7 6 5 4 3 2 1

EDITOR'S FOREWORD

The theory of prices and markets is at the heart of economics, and it is natural for a volume such as this to appear in a series of books on the principles of economics. Professor McKenna has given a readable introduction to one of the cornerstones on which the discipline has been constructed.

This volume is one of a series of short introductions to important topics in modern economics. The publishers and the editor have been impressed by the development of economic research over the past twenty years, and by the slowness with which many exciting new problems have become accessible to undergraduates and their teachers. It is not yet apparent which parts of this new research will become the backbone of teaching programs of the future, but it is clear that important changes will occur. The publication of a series of short, paperback volumes will permit instructors to experiment with new course material in areas where existing subject matter seems dated. Such a series also encourages the participation of young and active scholars in the development of new course material, without forcing them to write long textbook manuscripts. The series as a whole is designed to present a balanced presentation of new and traditional course material in such a way as to make it easier for instructors to introduce their students to the leading ideas and methods of modern economic thought.

Stony Brook, New York
January 1972

Edward Ames

PREFACE

As a teacher at all university levels, I have long felt the need for a basic handbook in price theory. Such a book should contain the elementary tools which every aspiring economist should know before moving on to applied economics or to more advanced tools of analysis. Supply and demand, marginal cost and marginal revenue, indifference curves and production isoquants, and the relationships among them are essential to know before examining more advanced topics. Nevertheless, it seems that many students reach even graduate studies without really understanding them.

This volume is intended to be such a handbook. It can be used as the basic framework for the microeconomics portion of an introductory course, supplemented with paperback volumes of applied economics, problem topics, or collections of readings. It can serve in an intermediate theory course, supplemented by detailed problems and by special topics which the instructor feels are appropriate. At the graduate level it can be the basic manual for an entrance examination to the advanced course. At my own university, we expect all graduate students to be able to answer *perfectly* any question drawn from this material and to reproduce correctly any of the diagrams.

Chapter 1 covers an introduction to the basic concepts of supply and demand and their elasticities. Chapters 2 and 3 deal with the consumer and the firm, respectively. These chapters use indifference curves and isoquants to derive demand and supply curves, and to demonstrate reaction to price changes. Chapters 4–7 examine the four major market types and demonstrate the different reactions of firms in each of these markets. Chapter 8 examines the labor market and derives the supply and demand for labor from the indifference curves and isoquants used earlier. (I have found such derivations lacking in most textbooks.) Chapter 9 is a reminder of the interaction process in the economy and the contrast between the market process and nonmarket decision making.

Throughout the book, the text and the forty diagrams have been carefully matched to permit correlation of the diagrammatic presentations and the verbal discussions. I have found this matching a great help to student understanding.

This book has drawn freely upon my earlier *Intermediate Economic Theory,* although many topics have been rearranged, some omitted, and substantial new material added.

Any author owes an immense debt to his family, who must bear with the disruption of their lives and listen to elaborate explanations as the author works out in his mind what he will include in the book. My wife, especially, has borne the brunt of this disruption, but she has performed her functions as critic, draftsman, typist, and general cheerleader expertly. In addition, I have pressed into service my daughter Celeste as typist and my son Kevin as draftsman. My special thanks to them.

St. Louis, Missouri
January 1972

Joseph P. McKenna

CONTENTS

A HANDBOOK OF PRICE THEORY

1

THE MARKET SYSTEM

Right now, as you read this, people in all portions of the world are busily working to prepare things which you will want. A plantation worker in Malaysia is tapping a rubber tree to collect sap which will ultimately become tires for your car. A worker in Hawaii is preparing pineapples, while a miner in Bolivia digs the ore which will become the tin lining on a can which will bring the pineapples to your home. Similarly, throughout our own country, workers in every state are anticipating your needs. This process works so effectively and so "automatically" that we never pause to think how wonderfully it works. Indeed, we accept it so naturally that we are apt to become quite indignant at even minor breakdowns, and complain to the manager if a store is temporarily out of our favorite brand of any product.

The mesh which keeps this enormously complicated system of production and distribution operating is called the market system, and the study of this system is the special field of the discipline known as economics. This study explains how the wide variety of raw materials and human skills which we call resources can be allocated to produce just the right amount of each of the thousands of products which people want and get them to the billions of separate recipients. Economics also examines the forces which cause the system to work less well at some tasks than at others, and why it sometimes suffers major breakdowns.

The principal mechanism used by the market system is a set of prices, which serve as a signalling device. Let us look briefly at the way that prices reflect changes in the system and help to produce desired results everywhere.

Let us suppose that a particular fad hits your campus, for example, the wearing of silk neckties with a hand-painted leaning tower of Pisa. (The fad was started because a campus leader, having received one from a slightly addled aunt, wore it to classes one day as a joke.) Shortly many students, men and women, begin to go to various tie stores looking for such ties. Only one store in town has any stock, a box of fifty purchased for reasons no longer clear to the manager. The manager, however, can clearly see that there are not enough ties to satisfy everyone, so he raises the price on the fifty he does have. He estimates that there must be fifty students who want to be "in" enough to pay a premium price. In fact, there are more than enough and the fifty are quickly sold. Since these ties are now the most profitable line in the store, the manager calls the manufacturer to get more. The manufacturer promises to send his own small stock immediately, and offers to produce more on a rush basis if the store will pay more than the usual wholesale price. The higher price will compensate for the extra costs of the rush order, overtime pay for cutting and sewing, extra bonuses for the artists, and possibly the extra wages required to lure some other artists away from other manufacturers. The extra ties are soon on their way to the store and are quickly sold at a price which is lower than the premium charged for the first fifty, but still more than the usual price for such ties.

Meanwhile, other merchants who also like money have not been idle. They have approached their suppliers to find some ties of this type. Since the original manufacturer can provide no more, other manufacturers, seeing the opportunity for extra profit, start to provide such ties. Soon everyone on campus is supplied, with prices continually dropping as the excess demand is satisfied. As the prices fall, no new orders are placed, and the tie industry drops back into its normal production pattern.

Thus we see that higher prices, representing more buyers of the product, passed the signal to other merchants and back to manufacturers. As the demand was satisfied, lower prices passed the signal that the extra production could stop and the situation returned to normal. Even in this rather trivial case, the price mechanism enabled the market system to adjust to the desires of the consumers.

However, there is still more to our story. The money which students spend on ties is money not spent on other goods. These goods tend to drop in price and less of them is produced. Wages of other workers may fall while the wages of artists rise, persuading some workers to shift jobs. In other words, the price mechanism passes on signals for less as well as for more.

On the consumer side, the price mechanism was also performing a service. It rationed the initial stock of ties to those who were prepared to pay the most for them, either because they had more money or wanted the ties more. It persuaded other students to wait until later to join the fad, until the prices came down to a level which they were willing to pay. (Notice that almost any student could have had one of the first ties if he had been willing to give up something else.) Thus the price mechanism is working constantly and simultaneously to adjust production to the desires of consumers and to adjust consumer purchases to the supplies available.

DEMAND AND SUPPLY

Economists have found that it is useful to describe markets by looking at supply and demand, and to represent these by particular curves. It should be borne in mind, of course, that supply and demand curves do not tell us anything we did not already know; they simply provide a way of organizing our knowledge into a more meaningful pattern.

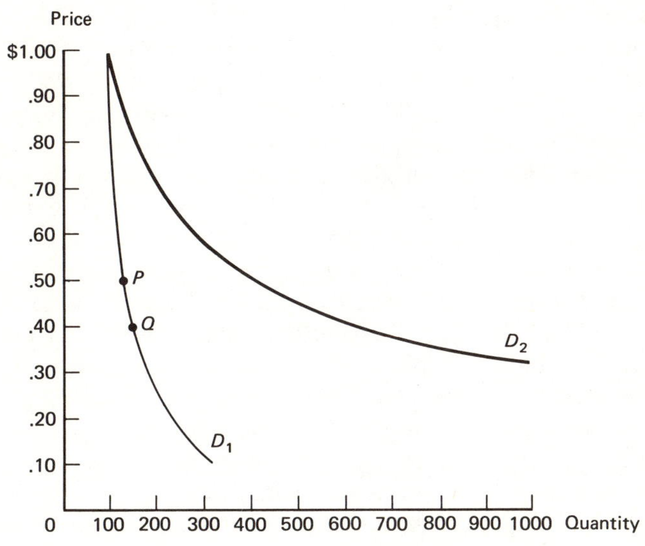

Figure 1.1 Demand Curves

Let us start with demand. At a particular price, consumers would usually wish to purchase a certain quantity of a particular good. If the price were higher, the potential purchasers would be fewer. If the price were lower, the quantity demanded would be greater. We can therefore say that typical demand curves look like those in Figure 1.1. They will slope downward to the southeast, although different demand curves will slope more or less steeply, and might be either straight lines or curves. However, it is almost always safe to assume, as we have here, that buyers will be willing to buy more at lower prices, and less at higher ones.

In order to avoid confusion later, let us agree to say that as price falls, there is an increase in the *quantity demanded.* When price rises, there is a decrease in quantity demanded. We will reserve the term, *increase in demand,* for the case when the entire curve shifts, causing a greater quantity to be desired at every price. Thus a change in *demand* means a *shift* of the curve; a change in *quantity demanded* represents a movement along the curve. In Figure 1.1, a movement from point P to Q is an increase in quantity demanded; the shift from curve D_1 to D_2 is an increase in demand.

It is useful to have a method of comparing two demand curves, and especially for measuring the response of quantity demanded to a change in price. The simplest measure would seem to be the steepness or flatness of the curve, its slope. Unfortunately, this would make the measurement of demand response dependent upon the units of measurement and the scale of the graph. A curve would be much flatter if the quantity were measured in ounces instead of pounds, and much steeper if measured in tons. To avoid this problem, we compare the *percentage* change in quantity with the *percentage* change in price. The ratio of these two percentages is called the *elasticity of demand.* For example, as the price is cut from \$0.50 cents to \$0.40, a 20 percent fall, the quantity demanded increases by 56 percent on D_2, but only by 12 percent on D_1. We can, therefore, say that the elasticity of demand at this price on D_2 is 2.8, but only 0.6 on D_1. D_2 is said to be an *elastic* demand curve, and D_1 is *inelastic.* The dividing line between these two is an elasticity of 1.0 (or unit elasticity). If the elasticity is one, the percentage fall in price will be exactly matched by the percentage increase in quantity demanded, and the total revenue will be unchanged. If the elasticity is less than one, the quantity change is smaller than the price change, so total revenue will fall as price falls, rise as price rises. If the elasticity is more than one, the quantity change outweighs the price change, so total revenue actually increases as price falls, decreases as price rises. Inelastic curves show the greatest total revenue at high prices, elastic curves the greatest revenue at low prices.

We usually refer to elasticity by the Greek letter eta, which is written η, and to change by the Greek letter delta, which is written Δ. For purposes of calculation we use the basic definition

$$\eta = \frac{\frac{\Delta q}{q}}{\frac{\Delta p}{p}}, \tag{1.1}$$

where p and q are price and quantity and Δp and Δq their changes. To simplify this rather involved fraction, we use the grade school rule for dividing fractions, which is to turn the denominator upside down and multiply:

$$\eta = \frac{\Delta q}{q} \times \frac{p}{\Delta p} = \frac{p\Delta q}{q\Delta p}. \tag{1.2}$$

Actually, this method of calculation is rather crude. Let us look only at D_2. If we had cut the price from \$0.50 to \$0.30, a 40 percent fall, quantity would increase by 178 percent, making an elasticity of 4.4. If we cut the price to \$0.20, a 60 percent decrease, quantity increases by 525 percent—an elasticity of 8.8. An 80 percent cut would lead to an elasticity of 30.0. (These last two cuts would take us off the diagram.) To avoid this difficulty, economists have agreed that the elasticity of demand should be calculated only on very tiny, even infinitesimal, price changes. Had we done this, we would find that D_2 has an elasticity of 2.0 and D_1 an elasticity of 0.5, not only at this point but everywhere. This limitation to infinitesimal changes does not mean that it will be necessary to pause for a course in calculus before continuing, for we will not need precise numerical estimates of elasticity. Our concern will be only with the general concepts of elastic and inelastic demand. We can use the numerical computation method given above as a crude measure, or simply check the effect of price change on total revenue.

Not all demand curves have the same elasticity throughout their length. We should, therefore, speak of a curve as elastic or inelastic at a particular point. When we do use the term *elastic demand curve*, we regard it as a short way of saying that the demand curve is elastic in the general region in which we are interested. Actually, most curves are elastic in some regions and inelastic in others. As an exercise, one can prove by careful measurement and calculation that a straight-line demand curve is elastic in the top half and inelastic in the bottom half.

Like the demand curve, the supply curve summarizes the reaction of changes in quantity to changes in price, but this time we are looking at the behavior of sellers, not buyers. We usually assume that the higher the price, the greater the quantity which sellers will offer. Many of the terms which we applied to demand curves can be applied to supply curves, with only modest changes. We use the term *change in supply* to designate a shift of the curve, and refer to movements along the curve as changes in *quantity supplied.* Similarly, we use *elasticity of supply,* and the same formula. However, since price and quantity change in the same direction, a unit elasticity no longer means a constant total revenue.

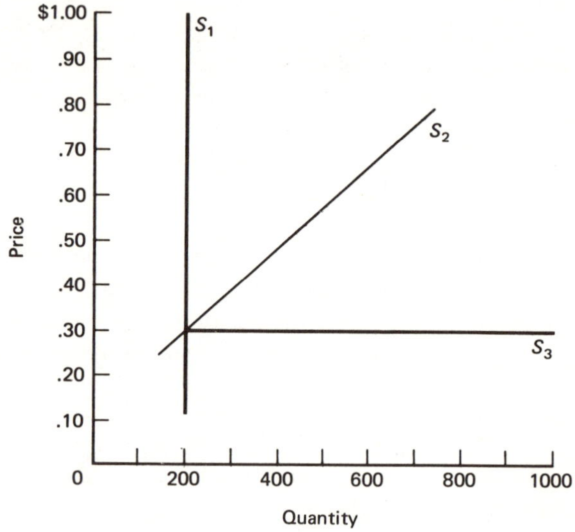

Figure 1.2 Supply Curves

Supply curves do not always slope upward. Figure 1.2 shows three types of supply curves. S_2 is the usual kind, indicating that a greater quantity would be supplied at a higher price. (Remember that the tie manufacturer demanded compensation for increased costs before providing extra ties.) S_1 represents the case where a fixed supply is available, no matter what the price. (Remember the immediate circumstances, when only fifty ties were available.) Finally, S_3 indicates a situation where any desired number will be provided, as long as the required price is offered.

Which of these supply curves is most appropriate to a particular case is often merely a matter of the time allowed for the response. The supply of most products is severely limited in the immediate period, so S_1 is the best representation. In a somewhat longer period, the quantity can be increased, but only if extra costs are incurred, so that higher prices are necessary, as represented by S_2. If a long period of adjustment is allowed, resources often can be shifted without extra cost, so that S_3 is most appropriate. Even if the shift is not costless, the result would tend to be closer to S_3 than to S_2.

The price which will prevail in the market is the price at which both suppliers and consumers are willing to trade the same quantity. In Figure 1.3, both supply and demand curves have been drawn on the same graph. Price P_1 is called the equilibrium price. At that price, sellers would be prepared to sell a quantity Q_1, and consumers would wish to buy the same quantity. Thus there are no buyers or sellers unsatisfied because they are unable to complete a desired transaction, and neither buyers nor sellers will try to alter the stated price. In economics, we call a position *equilibrium* if there are no forces tending to cause change from it.

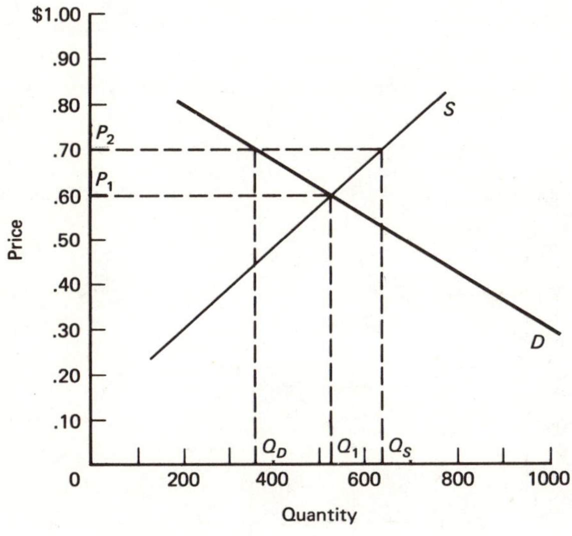

Figure 1.3 Supply and Demand

By contrast, P_2 is not an equilibrium position. Suppliers would wish to sell an amount, Q_S, which is larger than the amount, Q_D, which consumers are willing to buy. The difference between these two represents an excess of supply, sometimes called a surplus. The amount actually sold would of course be only Q_D, since no sale can take place without a buyer. Some of the suppliers, fearful that they will sell nothing at all, will offer to cut prices below P_2, in order to guarantee themselves a market. Thus we see that P_2 sets up forces tending to cause change, and therefore does not satisfy the definition of equilibrium.

If we started from a price below P_1, we would find that the quantity demanded is greater that the quantity supplied, causing an excess of demand, a shortage. Again, the amount traded will be the lesser of the two, the quantity supplied, since no purchase can take place without a seller. In this case, some of the buyers will offer higher prices, rather than run the risk of being left out.

Thus the only price which is an equilibrium position is P_1. Furthermore, since price will tend to fall from any higher position and rise from any lower position, P_1 is said to be a stable equilibrium. This means that a movement away from equilibrium will tend to be corrected, by moving back to the original price. Fortunately, most situations in economics have stable equilibrium solutions, but occasionally an unstable position occurs, so that errors are aggravated rather than corrected. We will meet such cases occasionally in this book, but it is generally safe to assume stability.

Let us now apply the tools of supply and demand to the case of the neckties. Initially, the supply curve is vertical, fixed at the fifty ties on hand. The high level of demand produces a high price, but no extra supplies. In Figure 1.4, this position is shown at P_1, the intersection of demand D_1 with the immediate supply, S_1.

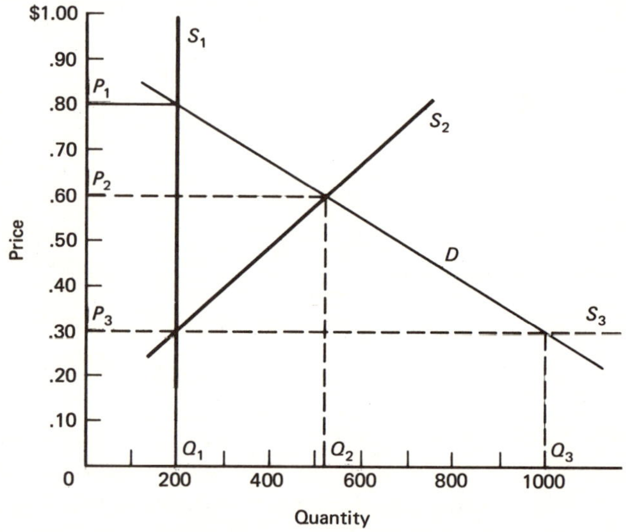

Figure 1.4 Market for Ties

As the merchant approaches the manufacturer and finds more neckties available at only somewhat higher prices than usual, the appropriate supply curve shifts to S_2. The price falls to P_2 and the quantity rises to Q_2. Finally, as other merchants and manufacturers begin to react, the supply curve shifts again to S_3. Price falls still further, to P_3, and quantity expands more, to Q_3. When the fad has run its course, there might be a downward shift of demand. Such a shift would drive prices down even further, but the quantity sold would be cut back. This shift is not shown in Figure 1.4, but you can test your understanding of these tools by representing the shift on a drawing of your own.

In the following chapters, we will look behind the demand curve at consumer behavior and behind the supply curve at the firm. We will then want to return to the market to examine further their interactions.

2

THE HOUSEHOLD

To understand better the role of prices in the market, we must look at households and at firms in more detail. The household is the economists' name for a consumer spending unit, which may be either a family or a single individual. Sometimes the spending unit is rather hard to define, as in the case of an unmarried worker living with his parents. Is he part of the same household, or a separate one? If most of his income goes into the family pool, he is considered a member of the family household; if he pays a sum for board and room, and spends the rest of his income for himself, he would be a separate houschold; between these cases are a wide range of possibilities, which are especially troublesome to statisticians trying to examine household behavior. We shall disregard these complications and assume well-defined family units.

The basic goal of the household is its own welfare, which includes physical satisfaction, social status, and all other dimensions of the good life. To avoid having to focus on the relative importance of these goals, economists have devised the concept of utility. *Utility is the measure of a consumer's welfare as he himself sees it.* It is, therefore, a compound of all those things that a consumer wishes, weighted as the consumer himself evaluates them.

The trouble with this definition is that it ends where it began. We say that households maximize utility, but we have defined utility as what households maximize. Thus almost any consistent behavior of a consumer is consistent with utility maximizing. A consumer may not behave "as I would have," but all he proves is that his utility maximization differs from mine. Most new automobile buyers purchase expensive models with lots of chrome, bright colors, excess power, and many accessories. They are obviously buying much more than transportation, but it is not our place to say that the sole purpose of an automobile is transportation. Moralists may object that people do not want what they should, but economists simply accept people's utility valuations and examine the effects. Since our principal concern is markets, we will focus on the way in which quantities purchased react to changes in prices and incomes. All other aspects are subsumed under the heading of utility.

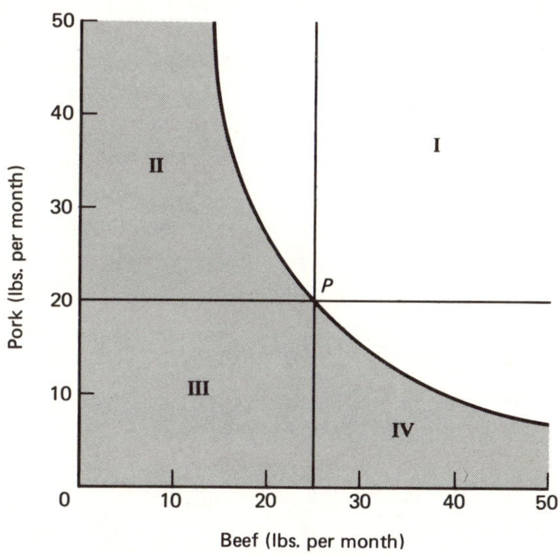

Figure 2.1 Indifference Curve

There remains one great difficulty with a catch-all concept such as utility: no easy measurement is possible. However, a crude measure is possible, and is enough for most problems we will want to discuss. We simply confine our measurement of utility to more or less, without trying to say how much. Let us imagine a household that is currently consuming twenty-five pounds of beef and twenty pounds of pork per month. This combination is shown as point *P* in Figure 2.1. It would clearly be better to have more of both meats, that is, to be at any point in the quadrant marked I. It would be worse to have less of both meats, as in quadrant III. The quadrants marked II and IV are not so clear. In these quadrants are the points that measure more of one good and less of another. Some of these points, in which a modest loss is compensated by a substantial gain, are better than *P;* others are worse. We can thus say that anything in the light area is better, while the dark area is worse. We have drawn in a line which divides the better area from the worse one. Any point on this curve represents a combination which is different from *P* but just as good. Since the household would consider all combinations on this curve equally satisfactory, it is called an *indifference curve.*

Naturally, if we had asked a different household to compare other points to *P,* we would have found a different curve, because few households have exactly the same tastes. Each indifference curve is merely a way of describing a particular set of preferences.

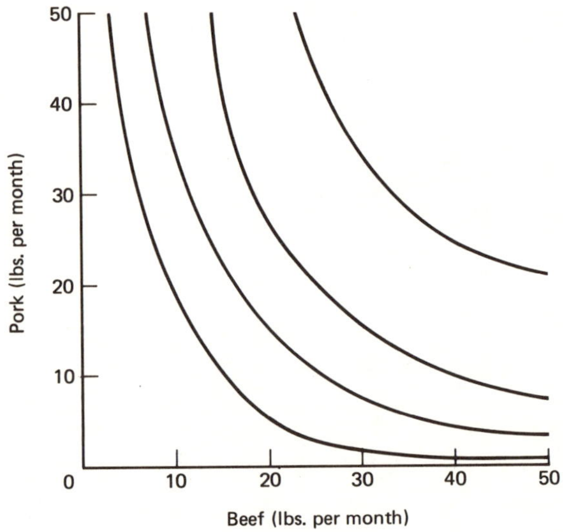

Figure 2.2 Indifference Map

Even for the same household, we could have found a whole set of indifference curves, called an *indifference map,* by using different starting points. Such a set is shown in Figure 2.2. Each curve, reading from left to right, represents a higher level of utility than those to the left. These curves are really contour lines of a three-dimensional model, on which utility is the altitude. Like contour lines on any map, these are chosen somewhat arbitrarily, and additional lines could be drawn between any two of these, simply by choosing a point between them and then finding other points equal in value.

Let us note a few important characteristics of this indifference map. Unlike ordinary contour lines, these have no numbers on them to designate the altitude. We know that indifference curves to the upper right represent higher utility, but we do not know how much higher. Occasionally we may assign numbers to them, but these are merely indexes for designation, not true measures.

We also notice that each combination of goods occurs on only one indifference curve. This is reasonable, for each curve represents a different level of utility, and no combination of goods has two different levels of utility. For the same reason, indifference curves cannot cross, for then the intersection would be on two curves.

The slope of an indifference curve at any point is called the household's *marginal rate of substitution,* the rate at which it is willing to substitute one product for another. We see that where the household has 40 pounds of pork and 15 pounds of beef, it will give up 7 pounds of pork for only 2 more pounds of beef, a ratio of 3.5 to 1. As the household gets more beef and less pork, it is less willing to make such a trade. When it has 25 pounds of beef and 20 pounds of pork, it will give up 5 pounds of pork only if it gets back 6 pounds of beef, a ratio of 5/6 to 1. The amount of curvature indicates the extent to which a household's marginal rate of substitution changes as it alters its consumption.

The marginal rate of substitution also shows us how commodities are related to each other in the market. Some commodities can easily be used to replace each other. This is especially true of different brands of the same product but also of different commodities. An automobile owner may find that additional motor oil consumption is a substitute for new piston rings. We call such products *substitutes,* and they can be identified by the small change in the marginal rate of substitution between them. The indifference curve representing perfect substitution is a straight line. (Perfect substitution need not be in a one-to-one ratio.)

At the other extreme are those products that go together in units. Such goods are called *complements.* Goods that are perfectly complementary are sold only in sets, like right and left shoes, because that is the way they are desired. Such products show a sharp break in the marginal rate of substitution at the right combination, since more of one would be useless without more of the other. Some goods are complementary, but not perfectly so. Gasoline and tires, for example, are complements, although not completely so; worn-out tires can be used a little more. An indifference curve showing perfect complementarity is L-shaped; where there is less complementarity, it is sharply angled. Complementary and substitutable goods are shown in Figure 2.3.

Most goods have some elements of substitutability and complementarity. All goods are substitutes, in that all produce utility and all compete for the same income. At the same time, all goods have elements of complementarity. In every social group, there are standard patterns of living that most members of the group follow. This standard pattern, then, constitutes the "right" combination, and the goods in this combination are complementary. These elements of substitutability and complementarity are blended, and this is indicated in Figure 2.2 by the fact that the indifference curves are neither the straight line of perfect substitutability nor the L-shape of perfect complementarity, but curved.

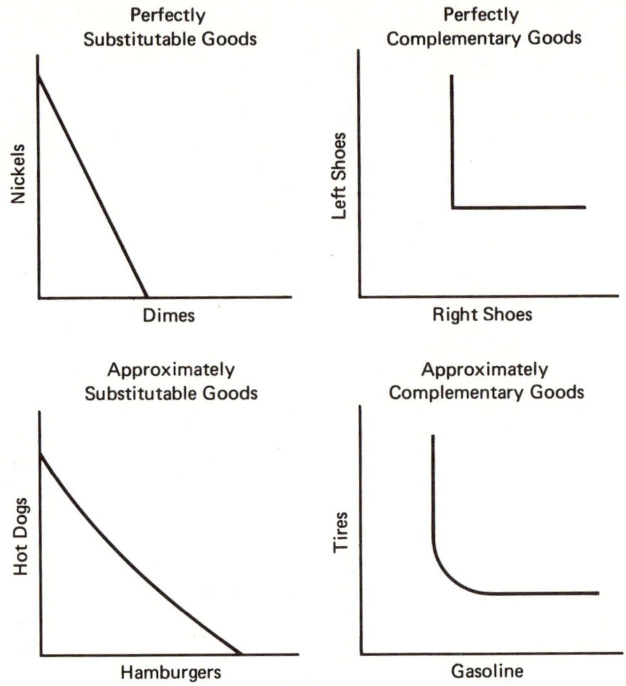

Figure 2.3 Substitutes and Complements

CONSUMER EQUILIBRIUM

A household has achieved an equilibrium position when it has done what it most wants, subject to the restrictions under which it must operate. The indifference map describes what a household would like; its income determines the limits within which it must operate. Let us consider how to add income information to the indifference map, assuming, for simplicity, that the household spends all its income on these two products. If the household has only \$18.00 to spend on meat, and beef and pork each cost \$0.40 per pound, its spending is limited by a rule:

$$0.40\,Q_P + 0.40\,Q_B \leq \$18.00. \tag{2.1}$$

In this inequality, Q_P and Q_B represent the quantity of pork and beef, respectively, that the household will purchase. The inequality itself says that the money spent on these two may not be more than the money available. If this household chose to buy only beef, it could buy up to 45 pounds. Similarly, it could buy up to 45 pounds of pork, or any combination of the two which did not exceed 45 pounds. In Figure 2.4 the area of possible choices is shown as the dark area in the lower left of the diagram.

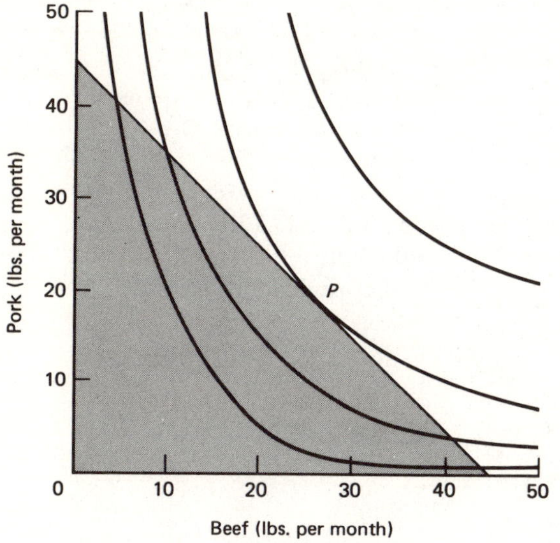

Figure 2.4 Consumer Equilibrium

This income limitation has been superimposed on the indifference map of Figure 2.2. As we look at the indifference map, we see that the household will almost certainly choose to spend its entire income, buying 45 pounds of meat and putting itself on the boundary line. A little study also indicates, however, that the household will try different combinations of the two meats until it finds the combination which is most satisfactory. Such a position occurs when the household chooses the point *P*, where it is consuming 20 pounds of pork and 25 pounds of beef. This combination puts the household on the highest possible indifference curve.

If a household actually knew the shape of its indifference curves, it would be a simple matter merely to compare the income restriction with the indifference curves and find the best position. Normally, such advance specification of preferences does not exist, because thinking about certain satisfactions and experiencing them are quite different. The way that a household tests its preferences is by a trial and error process of choosing various combinations and deciding which it likes best. This process of testing and experimentation is continuous, so that households may be said always to be approaching their equilibrium, without necessarily reaching it. However, with respect to common goods, it probably is safe to assume that households get close to their equilibrium position very quickly. In our further discussions, we will assume that this is the case.

At point *P*, the income line and the indifference curve are tangent, which means that they both have the same slope at this point. The slope of the income line depends upon the relative prices of the two meats, indicating the rate at which they can be exchanged in the market. The slope of the indifference curve, the marginal rate of substitution, reflects the relative utilities of the two goods. Thus, the equilibrium point occurs where the household has matched its own relative preferences to the market's relative valuation. As such adjustments take place throughout the society, every household will adjust until its relative preference also matches these price ratios, so that all relative valuations in the society will be the same.

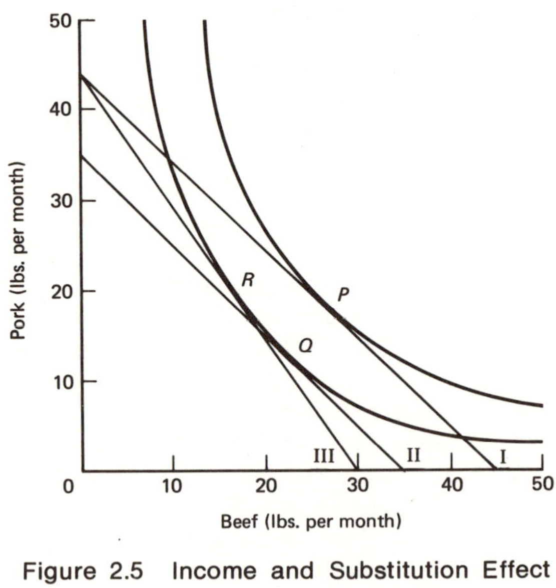

Figure 2.5 Income and Substitution Effect

If the household's income falls, so that it has only $14.00 to spend on meat, it will find itself with a new income line, represented by II in Figure 2.5. It can now buy only 35 pounds of meat, and its equilibrium is at *Q*, with 23 pounds of beef and 12 pounds of pork. This decline in income has led to a decrease in the purchase of both meats, the usual result.

If the household maintains its original income of $18.00, but the price of beef rises to $0.60, it must buy less. If it buys only beef, it can buy 30 pounds. It can buy beef and pork in the various combinations indicated by line III. It now finds its equilibrium position at *R*, with 16 pounds of beef and 21 pounds of pork. It would be spending $9.60 of its $18.00 on beef and $8.40 on pork. In its effect on the household's satisfaction, this increase in the price of beef is equivalent to the decline in income, for *Q* and *R* are on the same indifference curve. At *R*, however, the household has shifted away from beef, which has become more expensive, to pork, which is relatively cheaper.

When the price of beef rose from $0.40 to $0.60, the household moved from *P* to *R*. This movement is a combination of two effects. In the first place, the household is poorer. If it had been forced to cut its expenditures to $14.00, its utility would have fallen the same amount, the distance from *P* to *Q*. We call this movement from *P* to *Q* the *income effect* of the price change. It ordinarily means a decrease in consumption of both products. In addition to this virtual decrease in income, the price ratio of the two goods has changed, beef becoming relatively more expensive and pork relatively cheaper. This occasions a shift in consumption away from beef, from *Q* to *R*, which we call the *substitution effect* of the price change. It means less beef and more pork. When we put the two effects together, we see that both lead to a decline in beef consumption, but that the income effect decreases consumption of pork and the substitution effect increases it. In this case, the net effect is a slight increase in pork consumption, but other cases might show an increase, a decrease, or no change.

LUXURIES, NECESSITIES, AND INFERIOR GOODS

As income rises, the consumption of different kinds of goods will change. Ordinarily, consumption increases as income increases. We use this relation to income to classify goods as necessities and luxuries. A necessity is something that is required and will not be given up readily as income falls. Actually, few things are absolute necessities, but many are relative necessities, so their consumption declines less than proportionately to a decline in income. The converse of this definition is that consumption will rise less than income, for, if these necessities are purchased even at low incomes, there will be little increase at higher incomes. The consumption of luxuries, on the other hand, rises and falls even more than changes in income. As the index of the relation between income and consumption we use the *income elasticity of demand.* We previously used the concept of price elasticity, which measured the percentage change in quantity demanded caused by a given percentage change in price. The income elasticity measures the percentage change in quantity demanded occasioned by a given percentage change in income. If consumption increases proportionately with income, the income elasticity is one. If consumption increases more than proportionately, income elasticity is greater than one, and we call the product a luxury. If the elasticity is less than one, the product is a necessity. In Figure 2.6, we have drawn beef as a necessity and pork as a luxury. Using the same prices as before, $0.40 per pound for each meat, we have drawn in income lines for $10.00, $14.00, and $18.00. As income increases from $10.00 to $14.00, a 40 percent increase, beef consumption increases from 20 to 23 pounds, a 15 percent increase. The income elasticity of beef at this point is 15%/40% or 0.38. Since pork increases 140 percent, pork has an income elasticity of 3.5. As income increases from $14.00 to $18.00, an increase of 29 percent, beef consumption increases 9 percent, showing an income elasticity of 0.31, and pork increases 67 percent, an income elasticity of 2.3. Both of these examples indicate that beef is a necessity and pork a luxury. (Naturally, these conclusions apply only to this consumer's preferences, not to beef and pork generally.) As when measuring price elasticity, to be perfectly accurate we should use infinitesimal changes, but these are precise enough for our purposes.

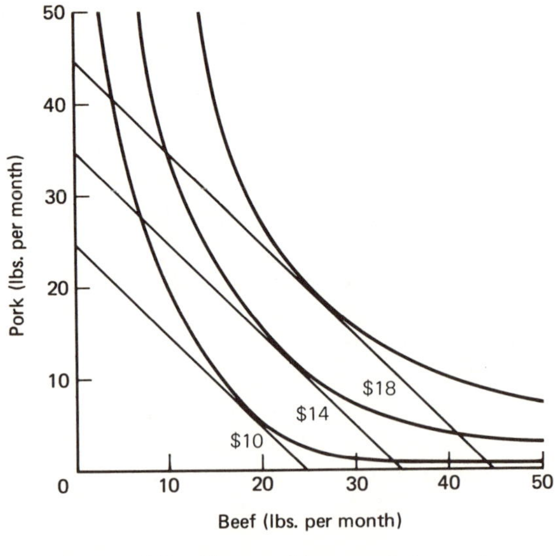

Figure 2.6 Necessities and Luxuries

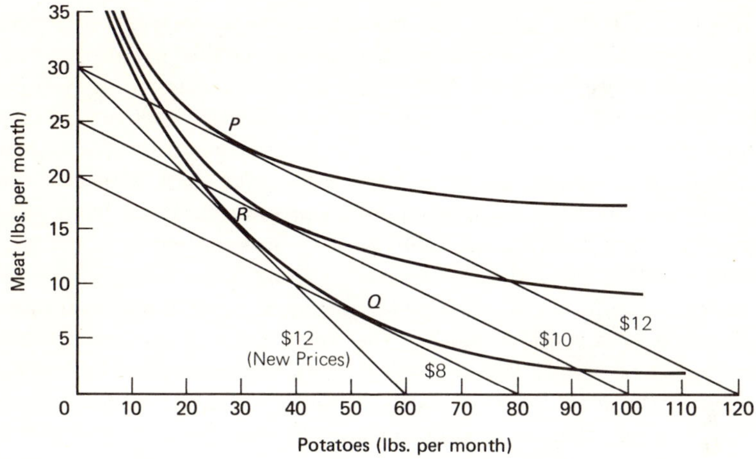

Figure 2.7 An Inferior Good

The definition of luxury and necessity in terms of income elasticity leads to certain surprising results. We find that cigarettes come closer to being an absolute necessity than any other product. They show less response to income changes than other products, and have an income elasticity near zero. Medical care, and especially dental care, are luxuries by this definition. If these conclusions do not agree with our views on how people should behave, it proves only that most people make more sensible decisions for others than for themselves. Our definition describes how people actually behave, not how they should behave.

There is a third class of goods known as inferior goods. These products are usually lesser substitutes for other products. As income rises, people may buy less of these inferior goods and shift to other and better ways to satisfy the same wants. Potatoes are an inferior good to the poor, who consume them as a cheap way to obtain necessary calories. As incomes rise, people buy fewer potatoes and more meat. They also buy other foods to add variety and taste. At higher incomes, oleomargarine and cheaper cuts of meat may be inferior goods, to be replaced by butter and steaks. Figure 2.7 shows several indifference curves and several income lines for an inferior good, in this example, potatoes.

Where a product is an inferior good, the income effect of a price change works backward. Let us consider the result of an increase in the price of potatoes. In Figure 2.7 we assumed an original price of $0.40 per pound for meat and $0.10 per pound for potatoes. At an income of $12.00 the household would consume 28 pounds of potatoes and 23 pounds of meat, settling at the equilibrium point *P*. If the price of potatoes rises to $0.20, the household finds its new equilibrium at *R*, with 8 pounds less meat and 1 pound more potatoes. As the price rose, the consumer bought more potatoes. We can understand this result by examining the income effect and the substitution effect. The income effect is represented by the movement from *P* to *Q*. Since potatoes are an inferior good, more potatoes and less meat are consumed at *Q*. The substitution effect is represented by the movement from *Q* to *R*, away from potatoes and toward meat. In this case, however, the income effect outweighs the substitution effect, and the net result is more potatoes and less meat. This unusual result is called *Giffen's paradox*, after the economist who allegedly first observed it among the Irish poor. It is now extremely rare, for today no single item constitutes a very large portion of consumers' expenditure. Few inferior goods, therefore, show a large enough income effect to outweigh the substitution effect.

INDEX NUMBERS AND UTILITY

The previous analysis of consumer behavior throws considerable light on certain problems of calculating index numbers. The Consumer Price Index presumably tells us something about what it costs consumers to maintain their standard of living. If we use the consumer's indifference curves to measure his standard of living, we can see how well it does this job.

Let us first consider the simple price index number. The usual method of calculation is by means of a weighted aggregate. This means that a standard bundle of goods is priced in two different years, and the index number is calculated as the ratio of the aggregate costs of the bundle in the two years. To make this index more realistic, the standard bundle is usually that actually purchased at some base period.

Let us return to our example of two meats. We saw that a household that had $18.00 for meat would buy 25 pounds of beef and 20 pounds of pork if the price of each were $0.40 per pound. Now let us imagine that beef rises to $1.00 per pound, but pork stays at $0.40. The same quantity of meat now costs $33.00, $25.00 for the beef, and $8.00 for the pork. The standard cost of living index for meat is $33.00/$18.00 or 183 percent. Actually, the household will not buy the same quantities of meat at the new prices, even if it has the $33.00. We can see from Figure 2.8 that, if the household were to spend $33.00 for meat, it would prefer to move from *P*, the old equilibrium, to *Q*, which is on a higher indifference curve. At that point it will buy 19 pounds of beef for $19.00 and 35 pounds of pork for $14.00. If will shift away from the more expensive beef and toward the less expensive pork.

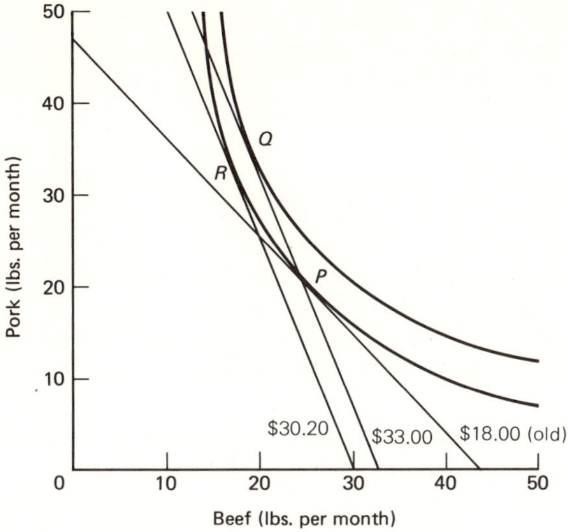

Figure 2.8 Cost of Living

The trouble with the standard index number is that it makes no allowance for the substitution effect. It tells how much it would cost to buy the same *goods,* not the same *utility.* If we really want to measure the cost of living, we should ask how much money would be required to maintain the same utility, that is, to stay on the same indifference curve as *P.* We find that point at *R,* which requires $30.20 for 17 pounds of beef and 33 pounds of pork. The true cost of living index is then $30.20/$18.00 or 168 percent, which is less than the 183 percent we calculated earlier. In practice, we have no way to determine these indifference curves and no way to calculate the true cost of living index, but we do know that it is always less than the standard weighted aggregate.

We can use the weighted aggregate *quantity index* to make certain inferences about utility. The usual method of comparing quantities is to compare the dollar value of the two bundles, measured at a single set of prices. One might use the prices of either last year or this year in comparing the purchases. Let us suppose first that we use this year's prices and find that the quantity index has risen. This means that the bundle of goods that the household bought this year costs more money than if it had bought the same bundle as last year. The only reason a family could have for spending more rather than less money is that the more expensive bundle is more desirable, that is, has a higher utility. We can, therefore, also conclude that the household is better off this year than it was last year.

Turning the argument around, if last year's bundle was more expensive at last year's prices, its utility was greater than this year's bundle, and the family was better off last year. Using p and q to represent price and quantity, the subscripts 1 and 2 to represent last year and this year, and Σ to represent the sum of all such items, we have two possible quantity indexes,

$$\frac{\Sigma p_1 q_2}{\Sigma p_1 q_1} \quad \text{and} \quad \frac{\Sigma p_2 q_2}{\Sigma p_2 q_1}.$$

The first of these uses last year's prices, the second, this year's. We conclude that the family was better off last year if

$$\frac{\Sigma p_1 q_2}{\Sigma p_1 q_1} \leqq 1,$$

for that would mean the household bought the more expensive bundle last year. We know the family is better off this year if

$$\frac{\Sigma p_2 q_2}{\Sigma p_2 q_1} \geqq 1,$$

that is, if this year's bundle at this year's price is greater than last year's bundle at this year's price.

Let us look at an example. Suppose that each month last year the family bought 17 pounds of beef at \$0.60 and 23 pounds of pork at \$0.30. This year it bought 25 pounds of beef at \$0.40 but only 20 pounds of pork at \$0.40. Can we tell when it was better off?

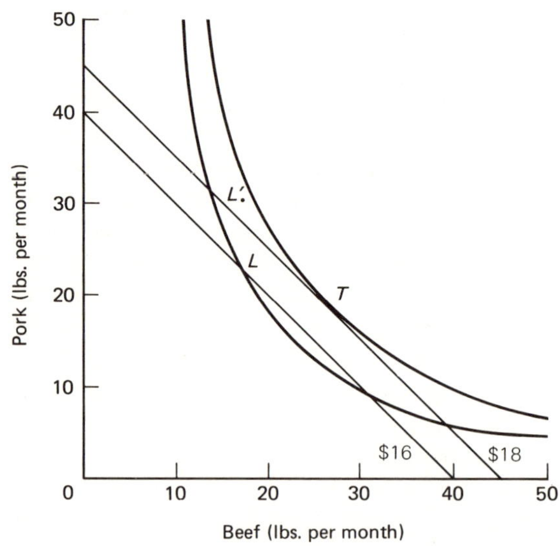

Figure 2.9 Improved Welfare

Last year the family spent $17.10 for the meat it bought. It would have cost $21.00 to buy the same as it bought this year. We cannot conclude anything from this, for they might have chosen the cheaper bundle either because it was cheaper, or because it was preferred.

This year the family is spending $18.00 per month, but it could buy the same meat it bought last year for only $16.00. That proves that it prefers the diet with more beef, for it could have the other diet and save $2.00. In Figure 2.9, we have indicated this year's bundle at *T* and last year's bundle at *L*. We have also drawn in the cost lines for this year, $18.00 and $16.00. We know that the $18.00 line must be tangent to an indifference curve at *T*, for that is the point the household chose. This indifference curve is always above the $18.00 cost line. The indifference curve passing through *L* must, therefore, be lower than the indifference curve through *T*.

Sometimes we find that the household chooses in each year the combination of goods that is cheaper that year. For example, suppose that last year it chose 19 pounds of beef at $0.60 and 27 pounds of pork at $0.30, shown in Figure 2.9 as *L'*. This year it chose 25 pounds of beef and 20 pounds of pork at $0.40 each. Last year it spent $19.50, but it would have cost $21.00 to buy this year's bundle. This year it spent $18.00 but it would have cost $18.40 to buy last year's bundle. Since it bought the cheaper bundle in each year, we have no way to tell which is better. As the indifference curves of Figure 2.9 are drawn, this year is slightly better, but we could draw indifference curves showing either bundle as the better one.

This device of inferring what a consumer's preferences must have been from his actual behavior is known as the principle of *revealed preference*. It is often a useful device for analysis of behavior, and is, in fact, the only satisfactory method economists have ever found to measure preferences. (We have already noted that most consumers do not really know what their preferences are until they are faced with an actual choice).

Another use of the principle of revealed preference is as a device for imputing meaning to changes in the gross national product of a country. For technical reasons which we will not discuss here, the measured gross national product in constant dollars is equivalent to a quantity index measured in this year's prices. If this index is greater than one, it is proper to assume an increase in consumer utility. This conclusion would be especially valid if the gross national product had been adjusted to per capita terms. There is, of course, a serious problem with distribution of income. If some people received more than their share of the increase and others actually received less, we would be unable to make any statement about the general welfare. If the gains were shared in reasonable proportion, we would be safe in assuming a general gain in utility from an increase in gross national product in constant dollars.

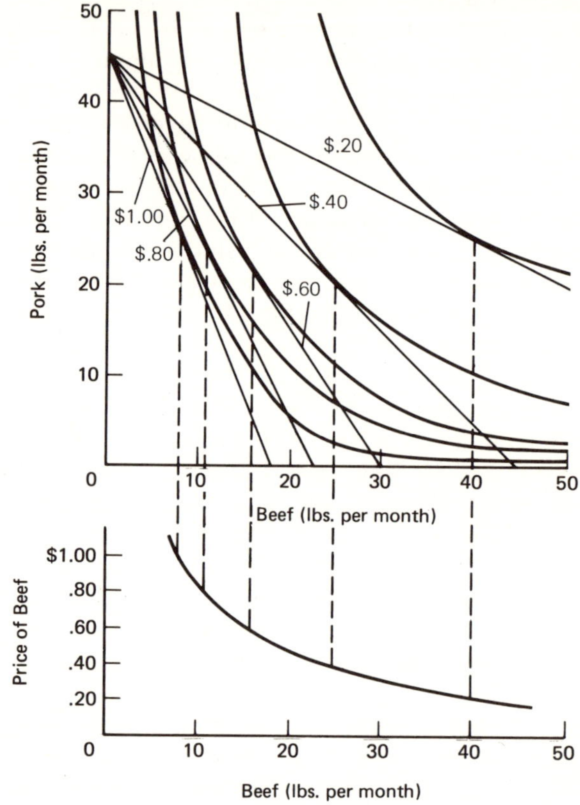

Figure 2.10 Demand for Beef

THE DEMAND CURVE

To find the household's demand curve for a product, we must find its equilibrium position at a number of different prices. Let us assume that a household's meat budget is fixed at $18.00, and that the price of pork is fixed at $0.40 per pound. We now wish to know how much beef will be purchased at each price. Let us start with a price of $1.00. We see that the highest utility comes with 8 pounds of beef and 25 pounds of pork, where the $18.00 spending line is tangent to an indifference curve. We have marked this line $1.00 in Figure 2.10, and plotted 8 pounds of beef opposite the price $1.00 in the bottom part of the graph. When we repeat this process for $0.80, we find the family consumes 11 pounds of beef. As we repeat this process for other prices, we find other equilibrium positions, each of which we plot on the bottom diagram. When we connect these points we have the demand curve for beef, other things being equal.

This last phrase is important. We have calculated the demand curve on the basis of a $0.40 price for pork and an $18.00 meat budget. If either of these were different, we would obtain a different demand curve for beef.

To give a more complete picture, we sometimes use total income and a composite demand for "all other goods" to determine total purchases of beef. This composite is usually measured in dollars and represents the best possible way of spending money for all goods except beef. Naturally, we assume that the prices of all other products remain unchanged while we focus our attention on the price of beef.

The demand curve we have just derived represents only the demand of a single household. When we discuss market behavior we want to know the total demand for that market. To obtain this demand, we add together the amount demanded at $1.00 by this household and by every other household to obtain the total amount demanded at $1.00 in the entire market. By performing this addition at other prices, we can derive the demand curve for the entire market.

3

THE FIRM

Just as the household is the general term given by economists to the typical consumer unit, so the firm is a designation given to producer units. However, there are much greater differences among firms than among households. A firm may be a single proprietor with no employees or a giant corporation with hundreds of thousands. It may be a simple producer of a single output or a firm with hundreds of separate products in its line. Despite their differences, all firms have certain similarities: they use certain resources and combine them to produce something which consumers want. In many cases, this something may be a specific product, like a refrigerator or an automobile. In other cases, the firm provides services, such as medical care, automobile repair, or haircuts. In the industries we call wholesale and retail trade, the firm buys products which others have produced and makes them available to consumers at times and in quantities which they desire. In each case, every successful firm provides something which has more utility to consumers than the materials it uses, and can therefore sell the product for more than it costs. This difference between costs and revenues is called profit, and it is a reasonable description of a firm to say that its goal is to maximize its profit.

It is clear that both revenues and costs depend upon many things, but we will concentrate first on their relationship with the quantity of product produced. The reason for this is that the critical economic decision processes in our society center upon the question of how much of each product is to be produced. We will also want to examine the way in which this quantity reacts to changes in prices, because we saw in Chapter 1 that prices were the principal signalling devices in our economy.

REVENUES

If a firm knew that whatever it produced could be sold at a certain price, then its revenue function would be a very simple one,

$$R = pq \tag{3.1}$$

where R is total revenue, q is the quantity produced and p is the constant price. On a graph of R against q, such a revenue function would obviously be a straight line. Many firms in our society do face such a revenue function, because they sell a standardized product in a market over which they have no control. Farmers, miners, and fishermen are usually in such markets. Notice that in each case they may not know in advance what the price will be, for this price depends upon the level of demand for the product at the moment and upon how much is produced by their competitors. The important thing, however, is that the price does not depend upon their own output, because each is too small a part of the market to make much difference by himself.

Many firms are not in this position. These firms are important enough in their own markets that they can increase the quantity which they sell by lowering the price. Most large firms face this condition, but so do many small ones; a neighborhood grocer is in this position because he occupies an important place in a very small market. These firms have the same revenue function, but p is no longer a constant. If such a firm wishes to increase its sales, it must realize that it will not increase its revenue by the full selling price of those extra sales; it must allow for the decrease in price on all its previous sales. For example, if a firm was selling 100 units at \$5.00, but must cut prices to \$4.99 to sell 101, the extra revenue will only be \$3.99—the \$4.99 it receives from the last unit minus the one cent it loses on each of the previous units. As a check on this calculation, we can multiply \$5.00 by 100, obtaining \$500.00, and compare it with \$4.99 times 101, or \$503.99. Again the increase is \$3.99. This increase in revenue from selling one more unit is called *marginal revenue*.

In most cases, of course, the calculation will not be made for one more unit, but for a great many. In such a case, one would find the marginal revenue by dividing the total increase in revenue by the increase in output. For example, if the firm was selling 100 units at $5.00 and could sell 110 units at $4.90, the marginal revenue would be $3.90. This amount could be obtained by subtracting $500 from $539 and dividing by 10, or by observing that each extra unit brings in $4.90, but bears one-tenth of the ten-cent loss on the previous hundred units. The formula for this marginal revenue is

$$MR = p - \frac{q\Delta p}{\Delta q}, \tag{3.2}$$

where p and q are the price and quantity and Δp and Δq are the changes in them. The second term of this definition indicates the loss on the previous quantity, divided by the increase in quantity.

As one would expect, the size of the marginal revenue is related to the elasticity of demand. In Chapter 1, we defined elasticity as

$$\eta = \frac{p\Delta q}{q\Delta p}. \tag{3.3}$$

If we rearrange Equation 3.2, we obtain

$$\begin{aligned} MR &= p - \frac{q\Delta p}{\Delta q} \\ &= p\left(1 - \frac{q\Delta p}{p\Delta q}\right) \\ &= p\left(1 - \frac{1}{\eta}\right). \end{aligned} \tag{3.4}$$

We see that if demand is very elastic (η is large) the marginal revenue will be close to the price, but as demand becomes less elastic the difference increases. When the demand becomes unitary ($\eta = 1$) the marginal revenue becomes zero, indicating that the increase in quantity barely compensates for the decline in price. If the demand is inelastic ($\eta < 1$) marginal revenue is actually negative, meaning the firm would have greater revenue if it sold less at a higher price.

If a firm knew exactly the shape of its demand curve, it is clear that it could construct a total revenue function which corresponded to it. More commonly, the firm is only sure of one position, that at which it has been operating. Exactly what would happen if the firm shifted to a different output (and price) is a matter for conjecture. Presumably a better guess is possible with respect to larger firms, but there are uncertainties involved. This explains why there are often disagreements among the officers of a given firm on whether to lower prices and try for higher volumes, and also why different firms in the same industry follow different policies. Often a firm will take modest steps to probe consumer reactions as a device for testing the exact location of the revenue function. We can also see why such problems provide great opportunities for market research firms who try to answer questions of "What would happen if . . . ?"

COSTS

Before we can compare costs with revenues, we must be sure of what is meant by cost. The simplest definition includes all money paid or payable in order to carry out a particular operation. This is essentially the definition used by accountants, who have devoted much thought and study to methods of measuring it accurately. Their most difficult problems involve dividing a single payment into the costs of different items. A machine may run for ten years; how much of its value is a cost this year? Many ingenious answers have been given to this and similar questions, but the basis of all these answers is the original cash payment.

Complicated as it is, this definition of cost is still too simple for our purposes. Every economic action involves a choice between alternatives. The true cost of any action is what one has given up for it. This is not always the same as the cash expenditure. (Every student knows that the cost of a movie during exam week may be two dollars plus ten points on his final grade.) Employing this definition of cost to interpret the firm's decision, we see that the proper cost is the *opportunity cost,* the value of the alternative that has been foregone to produce a certain output. In many cases, this is the same as the market price, for all that one has given up to use, say, an extra pound of aluminum, is the price of that pound. As long as these goods are bought in the market and readily available, this will be the case. In fact, the market price does reflect the opportunity cost, for one user must outbid another so that the latter will pass up his opportunity.

For inputs that are not purchased currently in the market, the price is no longer a satisfactory measure of cost. Foremost among these nonmarket inputs are those provided by the owner. The man who works in his own firm does not incur a cash expense, but there is certainly an opportunity cost; he might otherwise be working for a salary. Similarly, any of his own money devoted to the business might have been loaned out at interest. It is customary to call these nonmarket costs *implicit costs,* and the market costs *explicit costs.* To understand the process of decision making in the firm it is necessary to include both implicit and explicit costs.

A second difference between market price and opportunity cost occurs if there is a long time lag between the purchase of an input and its use.

At the time of purchase one gives up exactly the market price to obtain the input, so the market measures opportunity cost. If there has been an important shift in price or change in technology since purchase, this will no longer be true. If similar inputs are now more expensive, the opportunity cost is higher, for this one might be sold at the new price instead of being used. This problem is obviously most important in measuring depreciation charges and inventory changes, for these are the cases where the intervals between purchase and use are longest. The same problem occurs in evaluating rent payments on a long-term lease.

From this discussion, it is clear that opportunity cost is not a single, unvarying number, but will change constantly with the alternatives available. If an owner would otherwise be unemployed, his opportunity cost might be very low. If the location of leased property has become more popular, opportunity cost will rise. Thus, opportunity cost is often shifting and usually difficult to evaluate.

The accountant usually deals mainly with explicit cost and market price valuation. There are various reasons for this, but the most important one is measurability; it is desirable to have invoices and receipts to depend upon. The accountant is the financial historian of a company and prefers to keep this record as objective as possible. (There are other reasons. Imagine the difficulties of the poor accountant who is called upon to evaluate how much his employer could earn in the open market.)

Many accountants have recognized the inadequacy of the purely historical record. Since the range of interpretations of opportunity cost is often quite wide, most of them adopt a compromise. They keep the official books of record on the basis of explicit, historical cost, but supplement these books with special reports that utilize a concept much closer to that of opportunity costs. Some of the methods initially developed in these special reports have found their way into the formal books of account. Most of the accounting discussions about replacement-cost depreciation and "last-in, first-out" inventory valuation can best be understood as methods of approximating opportunity cost.

Costs can also be divided into *fixed costs* and *variable costs.* Since our primary concern is the cost–output relationship, we will designate as fixed those costs that do not change as output changes, and as variable costs those that do. Fixed costs may vary with time, or with other changes; they are fixed only with respect to output. Rent is a fixed cost, although with a capricious landlord, it might change from month to month. Most wages are variable costs, but, with a union contract and stable production, they may remain constant for a long period. Some wages, such as those of executives and key personnel, are fixed costs, because these people are employed no matter what the level of production.

In any company with a true guaranteed annual wage, wages become a fixed cost, no longer depending upon output, at least over wide ranges. Raw material costs are mostly variable costs, but depreciation is a fixed cost unless additional use accelerates the wearing-out of the machine. A convenient rule is that fixed costs are those which would continue even if output were zero, and variable costs are everything else. This rule is inadequate because there are really two kinds of fixed costs. Some of them continue because they are contractual and would go on even if the firm were bankrupt. Others continue as long as the firm remains in existence as an operating business, even though temporarily shut down. For most purposes, we will want to include both as a part of fixed cost, although some decisions depend only on the contractual costs. Ordinarily, we will use fixed costs to mean those that would continue during a temporary shutdown.

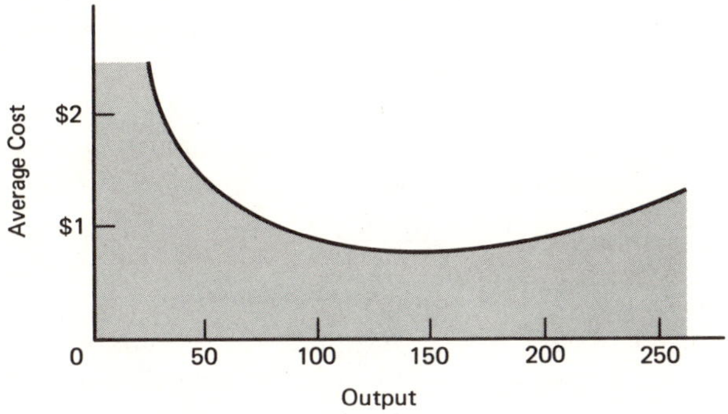

Figure 3.1 Cost Region

What it costs a firm to manufacture a given quantity of output is apt to be a rather uncertain amount. It depends upon the techniques in use, but also upon the effectiveness with which the management uses the facilities which are available. Economists often refer to "the cost curve" of a firm, but it is clear that there is really a region of costs, rather than a specific cost for each output. In Figure 3.1 a cost region is shown as the white area of the diagram. Any cost above the shaded region might be the cost of producing a given output by a given firm. Naturally, the more efficient the firm, the closer it will be to the shaded area, but there is an absolute lower limit to costs of production with given technology. Only a new invention or technique would make it possible to achieve a cost in what is now the shaded area.

We might consider the boundary line, which divides the possible costs from the impossibly low ones, as the cost curve of a firm, in the sense that it represents the lowest possible set of costs. In this sense, "the cost curve" is an ideal which real firms may seek, but few actually reach. We will discuss certain aspects of reaching this minimum in a later section.

Because most firms are merely seeking their minimum cost without actually achieving it, and guessing at their revenue function without knowing it, we should be rather surprised if many firms actually maximized profits. Indeed, what many of them seem to do is find a satisfactory position and then stay there. However, better-managed firms use the satisfactory position only as a base for possible changes. Even the less efficient firms will find that competitive pressures are apt to force efficiency upon them, under threat of bankruptcy.

If a firm wishes to decide whether a given change will make its position better or worse, it must compare the gains from that change against its costs. We have already defined the changes in revenue as marginal revenue, and seen how they relate to the shape of the demand curve. In a comparable way, we can define *marginal cost* as the increase in cost associated with producing one more unit. If marginal revenue exceeds marginal cost, there is a marginal profit, that is, profit can be increased by making the change. It would therefore pay the firm to increase its production if marginal revenue is greater than marginal cost, and to cut back production if marginal cost is greater. Since marginal costs of firms tend to increase with greater output, and marginal revenues tend to decline, a firm can keep expanding its output until marginal revenue crosses marginal cost. This is often summarized by saying that the point of maximum profit occurs where marginal cost equals marginal revenue, which would be the case if output were perfectly divisible. In general, it is perhaps better to think in terms of inequalities: expand if marginal revenue is greater than marginal cost, contract if it is less.

INPUTS AND COST: ONE VARIABLE INPUT

An input whose quantity the firm can vary at will is called a variable factor of production; an input that cannot be increased (or, in some cases, decreased) is a fixed factor. Suppose that a farm of 10 acres with one man working on it produces 500 bushels of output. If these are the only factors of production, one would naturally expect 1000 bushels from a similar farm of 20 acres worked by two men, 1500 bushels from a 30-acre, three-man farm, and so on. Naturally, one would not expect such proportionate increases in output if only one factor, say, labor, were increased. We would, therefore, not be surprised if the 10 acre farm produced only 700 bushels with two men or 800 bushels with three. This rather obvious fact has been enshrined in economics as the *law of diminishing returns*. This law states that, as more of a variable factor is applied to a fixed factor, the output increases less than proportionately. In fact, it is even possible for the net increase to become negative. This will occur when there are so many men on the farm that they get in each other's way.

As economists continued their study of actual economic activity, it became clear that it would occasionally be necessary to revise this law. In some circumstances, an increase in variable factors increased the output more than proportionately. This unexpected result occurred because the fixed factor might originally have been used past the point of negative returns. Imagine the results if one man were trying to farm several thousand acres. He might actually increase his output by concentrating on less of the acreage. Unfortunately, some fixed factors are not easily divisible, so one must use all of them, even if they are too big for the labor force. (Operating an assembly line with a few workers may be the most inefficient way possible of producing automobiles.) All these observations indicated that there might be an initial period of increasing returns, and the rule became the *law of eventually diminishing returns.*

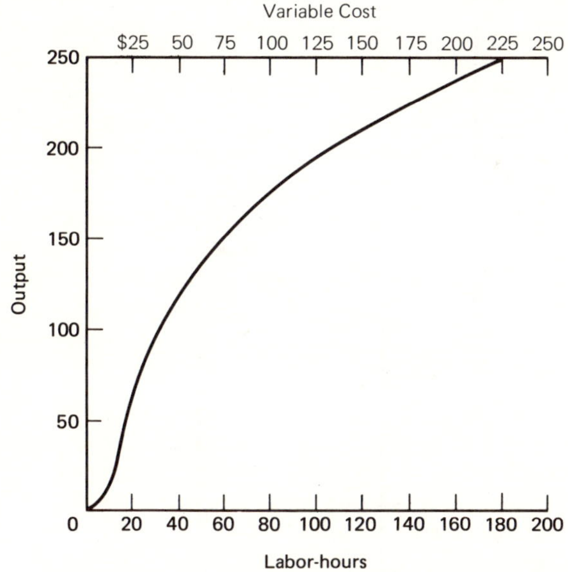

Figure 3.2 Production and Variable Cost

Most cost curves drawn by economists reflect this law of diminishing returns. If production is subject to first increasing and then decreasing returns, the graph of output against input will rise steeply at first, flattening out as diminishing returns set in. Such a curve is shown in Figure 3.2. Since there is only one variable factor of production in our example, all the elements of variable cost are implicit in this graph. We can change this purely technical relationship into a variable cost curve by multiplying the input by its price. In this example, we have assumed that labor costs $1.25 per hour, so the top scale of Figure 3.2 represents the variable cost of producing each output. For example, it takes 32 labor hours to produce 100 units of output. At $1.25, this labor will cost $40.00. The variable cost of producing 100 units is, therefore, $40.00.

Since we are often interested in the total cost rather than just the variable cost, we add the fixed cost to the variable cost. If we assume that the fixed cost is $50.00, the total cost of production of 100 units is $90.00, $50.00 of fixed cost and $40.00 of variable cost. This addition is shown in the upper part of Figure 3.3. We have reversed the axes, putting output on the horizontal scale and cost on the vertical scale. There is no compelling reason for this reversal, but this is the customary usage among economists, so we will adhere to it.

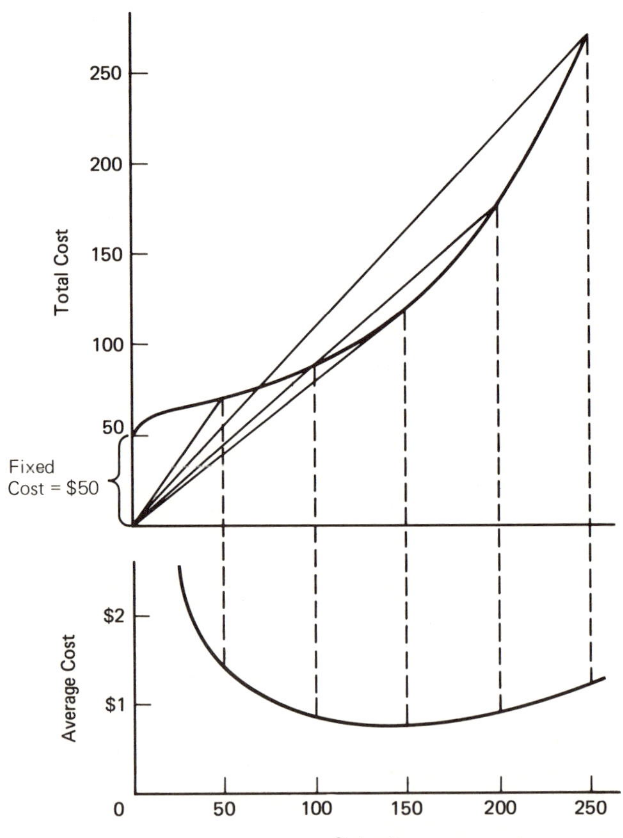

Figure 3.3 Total and Average Cost

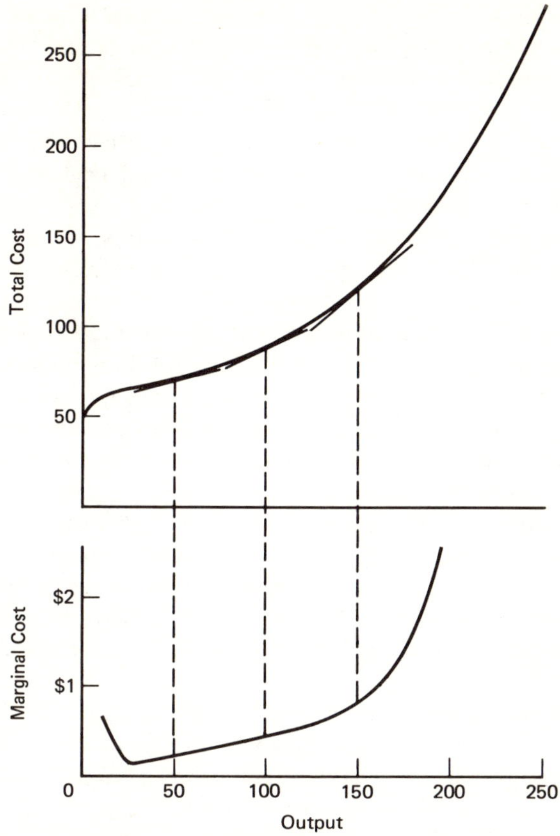

Figure 3.4 Total and Marginal Cost

From the total cost curve of Figure 3.3, we can obtain average cost and marginal cost curves. Since average cost is total cost divided by output, it can be obtained geometrically by dividing the height of the total cost curve at any point by its horizontal distance from the vertical axis. These two distances form the legs of a right triangle whose hypotenuse extends from the zero point to the total cost curve. The average cost is the tangent of the angle at zero—the ratio of the lengths of the vertical to the horizontal legs of the triangle. For example, at an output of 200 units, the total cost is $180.00. Average cost is $180.00/200 or $0.90. For our purposes, it is sufficient to note that the larger this angle and the steeper this line to the origin, the higher the average cost. The lowest average cost will therefore come at the point where the line is flattest, in this case at 150 units.

A similar construction can be used for the marginal cost, as shown in Figure 3.4. The marginal cost is measured by the increase in cost, that is, by the steepness of the curve between successive units of output. If these units are close enough together, this steepness can be measured by the straight line which is tangent to (just touches) the curve at any point. (We see, for example, that the tangent at 150 units increases $80.00 per hundred units, so that the marginal cost is $0.80.) By comparing the two diagrams, we see that the marginal cost and the average cost are equal at the minimum average cost. In Figures 3.3 and 3.4, this occurs at an output of 150. At outputs less than this, marginal cost is less than average cost. This means that average cost is falling, since each additional unit adds less than proportionately to the total. At greater outputs, marginal cost exceeds average cost and average cost is rising.

Similar diagrams could be drawn to show total, average, and marginal revenues. Since the demand curve represents average revenue, we would have to construct a total revenue curve by multiplying price and quantity of the demand curve. Marginal revenue can then be drawn by following the model of Figure 3.4.

As we have noted before, not all firms are efficiently managed. We should therefore regard the production curve of Figure 3.2 and the cost curves of Figure 3.3 and 3.4 as boundary curves. Many firms will get less production from a given output than shown in Figure 3.2 and will consequently have higher costs for every unit of output than shown in Figures 3.3 and 3.4.

This description of cost is sufficient if there is only one variable input, which may be the case with short-run decisions in many firms. In most small retail operations, even labor may be a fixed cost, and the size of the inventory may be the only variable cost. For some firms, however, both labor and materials are variable, and we must use a more complex form of analysis. If we allow a comparatively longer period of time for adjustment, no firm fits the simple one-variable model. Given enough time, any firm can vary the size of its plant, machinery and labor force.

The possibility of altering fixed costs is the criterion economists use to distinguish between short run and long run. In the *short run,* the firm may adjust its scale of production, but only within the confines of its present plant structure. In the *long run,* firms may buy new equipment or sell old, and new firms may be started or old ones leave the industry. In the long run, there are no fixed factors, and adjustments of all kinds may take place.

There is no specific length of time that divides short run from long run. In some lines of production, long run may be as little as three months, for a firm might be able to add machinery in such a short period of time. In other industries, long run might mean years. Such would be the case in some kinds of mining, where elaborate preparation is necessary before opening a new vein. Furthermore, the time may be different for expansion than for contraction. Machines that can be installed in months may take years to wear out. If they are so specialized as to have little second-hand value, then long run may mean years for contraction. In the textile industry, for example, there are too many plants. Many of these are obsolete but not worn out. Eventually, they will be closed down, but meanwhile there can be no complete adjustment in the textile industry. Similarly, most students of the farm problem agree that the principal difficulty is that there are too many farmers for peacetime conditions, but farmers do not like to leave their industry and move to town. Here too the long-run adjustment may take many years.

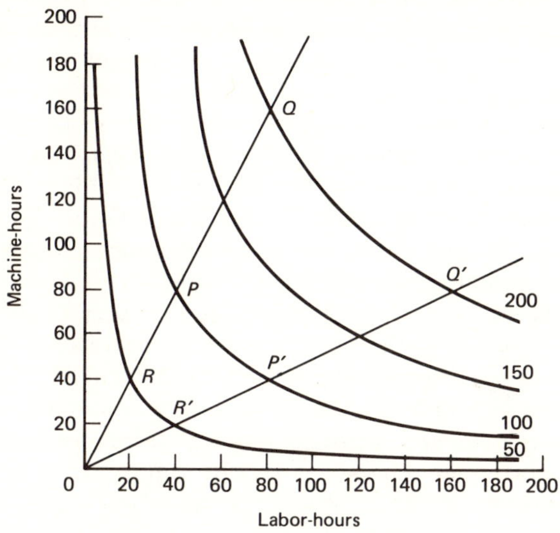

Figure 3.5 Production Function

INPUTS AND COST: TWO VARIABLE INPUTS

We can examine the choice of inputs where two are variable by a technique similar to the one which we used to examine consumer behavior. In Figure 3.5, we represent the possible combinations of inputs and output by a three-dimensional diagram with the two inputs and one output on the axes. In order to reduce these three dimensions to a two-dimensional page, we will use contour lines for the third axis, the output. On the two axes, we list quantities of the two inputs, in this example, man-hours and machine-hours. We draw a curve through all combinations of these two inputs that can be used to produce a particular output, say, 100 units. We see, for example, that this output can be produced with 40 hours of labor and 80 machine hours, or 40 machine-hours and 80 man-hours, or with many other combinations. Other curves can be drawn to represent other outputs, such as 50, 150, or 200 units. Since each of these curves represents a particular level of output, they are called equal-product curves or *isoquants*. The similarity to the consumer indifference map of Figure 2.2 is obvious.

Like the indifference curves of Chapter 2, the exact shape of these isoquants is often not known by the firm. It often must do some trial and error rearranging of its production in order to find their exact shape. However, engineering studies and trade journals often help the firm to make better decisions, since these are essentially technical questions, and answers learned in one firm can be used in another. (By contrast, consumer preferences are unique. The experience of one consumer is of little help to another.)

Since we have assumed that there are only two factors of production, the isoquants show complete proportionality. Every point on the 200 curve uses exactly twice as much labor and machinery as the corresponding point on the 100 curve. This is demonstrated by points P and Q. To produce 100 units at P, we need 40 hours of labor and 80 machine-hours; to produce 200 units at Q, we need 80 hours of labor and 160 machine-hours. Points P' and Q' also show this proportionality. Similarly, every point on the 50-unit output curve uses half as much of each input as the corresponding point on the 100 curve. The output at R uses 20 labor-hours and 40 machine-hours, half as much as at P. Point R' uses half as much of each factor as point P'. Since points P, Q, and R represent proportionate changes in both inputs, they fall on a line through the origin. P', Q', and R', representing another proportion, fall on another line.

When the production function has this property of proportionality, we say that it is *homogeneous*, or, more precisely, homogeneous of the first degree. This property of homogeneity means that an equal percentage increase in each input will cause an increase of the same percentage in the output.

The case we discussed earlier, of one fixed and one variable factor, is merely a special case of this one, as shown in Figure 3.6. Let us assume some particular amount of machine-time available, say 80 hours. Reading horizontally across the graph at this point, we see that we would require about 13 man-hours to produce 50 units. To produce 100 units would require about 40 man-hours. One hundred fifty units require 88 man-hours and 200 units require 160 man-hours. In the bottom half of Figure 3.6 we have plotted the outputs against the number of labor-hours required, which results in a production curve similar to that of Figure 3.2.

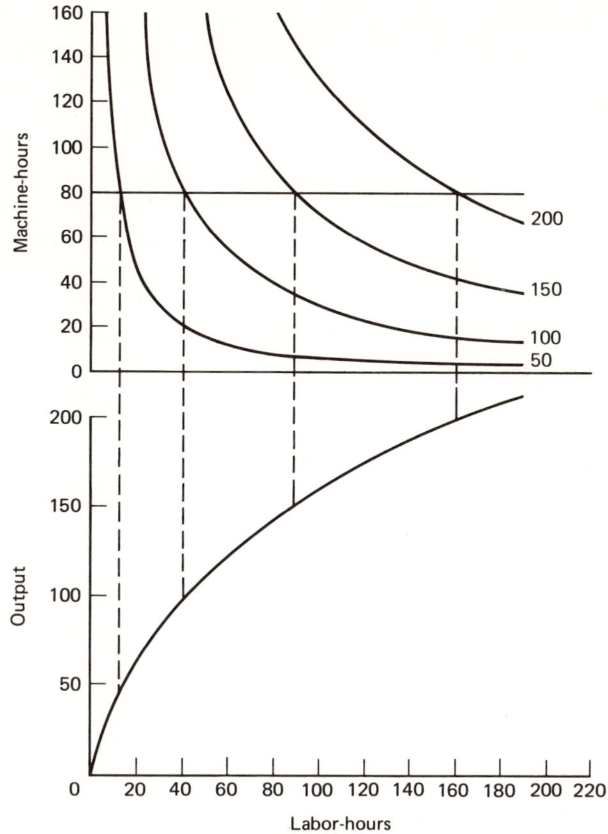

Figure 3.6 Fixed and Variable Factors

So far, we have discussed various ways of producing any given output. We have not yet considered the cost of producing by these various combinations. To do so, we need to know the costs of the factors of production. We said at the beginning of this chapter that the raw data of our problem are the technical conditions of production and the market supply of the factors. Here we will assume that the supply conditions are such that the firm can hire all the labor and machinery it wants at \$1.00 per hour for men and \$0.50 per hour for machines. In such a case, we can list all the combinations of factors of production we can hire for a given sum. For \$40.00, we could hire 40 hours of labor and no machines, or 80 machine-hours and no labor, or 40 machine-hours and 20 labor-hours. Since we have assumed that both of these prices are fixed, each equal-cost line will be a straight line. In Figure 3.7, we have drawn a set of possible equal-cost lines at forty-dollar intervals, superimposed on the isoquants of Figure 3.5. The firm can now search for the lowest cost combination of inputs for producing a given output, say 100 units. After some trial and error, it will find that point at P, where the 80 machine-hours and 40 labor-hours will cost $80.00. Every other point on the isoquant would involve a higher cost. At this minimum cost point, the equal cost line and the isoquant are tangent and have the same slope. (Note that the firm has equated its marginal rate of substitution for the inputs with the price ratio, the market rate of substitution. Again the similarity to consumer behavior is obvious.)

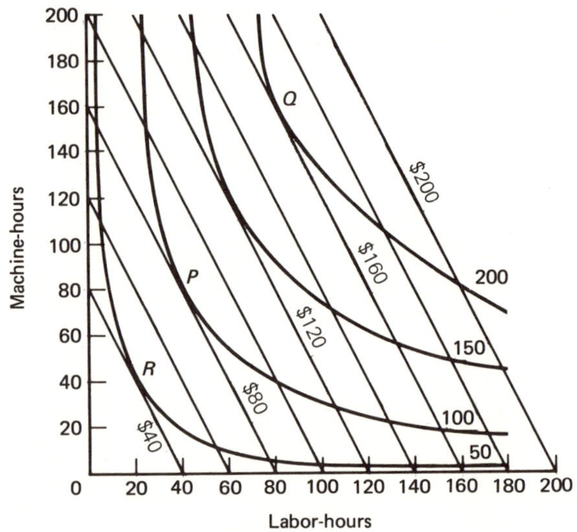

Figure 3.7 Equilibrium Combination

Since we assumed that the production function is homogeneous, we would expect the least-cost combination for other outputs to be proportional to the combination for 100 units. If we refer again to Figure 3.7, we see that this is indeed the case. The least-cost combination for 200 units is at *Q*, with twice the labor, twice the machines, and twice the cost of producing 100 units at *P*. The best way to produce 50 units is at *R*, with half as much of everything as at *P*. Thus we find that, if we assume proportionality in the production function, increases in output also cause proportionate increases in cost. The total cost curve is therefore a straight line starting from the zero point. The average cost and marginal cost curves would both be horizontal lines, in this case at $0.80 per unit.

If there are fixed factors as well as these variable factors, the production function will no longer be homogeneous and the law of diminishing returns will again apply. In such a case, the total cost curve would no longer be a straight line, but would probably have a shape rather like that of Figure 3.3.

It is probable that the nonhomogeneous production function is far more common in practice than the homogeneous one. Almost every firm has some "lumpy" factors of production that are not fully variable. These factors may be available only in very large units and therefore not capable of very precise adjustment. Automobile assembly lines and steel blast furnaces are examples. Over a wide range of output, the firm might not change the quantity of such factors and therefore they are treated as fixed.

Whatever the variability of physical units of production, management is a fixed factor. Changing managers is not a complete solution, for it still introduces a lumpiness like that of large, indivisible, physical plants. In order to use a very good manager to full capacity, a very large scale of operations may be required. If this is true, there will be a rather large area of increasing returns, due to the "large" input, before diminishing returns set in.

CHANGE IN INPUT PRICES

The cost curves we have just derived are based upon a particular set of prices, in this case $0.50 per hour for machines and $1.00 per hour for labor. When a firm uses these costs and its revenue function to determine the best output, that choice of output depends upon the factor prices. Any change in factor prices would alter the choice. Let us look at this change in more detail.

Let us assume that the firm has chosen to produce 150 units of output at the old costs. The cheapest way to produce this output requires 120 machine-hours and 60 labor-hours, at a total cost of $120.00. The equilibrium point is shown at *P* in Figure 3.8. The $120.00 cost curve is shown by the dotted line. Now let us imagine an increase in machinery prices to $1.50 per hour. The new equal-cost lines will be much flatter than the old ones. Some of these have been drawn in. It now costs $240.00 to produce at point *P*, for the machinery cost has increased to $180.00. Naturally the firm will reconsider its production techniques and tend to substitute labor for the machinery. It finds that its least-cost combination for producing 150 units is now at point *S*, at a cost of $210.00. Although this is less than the $240.00 it would cost to remain at *P*, it is more than the old cost of $120.00. Substitution always avoids some of the effects of the price increase, but not all of them, for as long as we use any machinery, the increase in its price will affect the total cost of production. We call this movement from *P* to *S*, as machinery prices rise, the *substitution effect* of the price increase. The substitution effect always involves a movement away from the factor that has become relatively more expensive and toward the factor that has become relatively cheaper. In the present example, we use 60 hours more of labor and 60 hours less of machines.

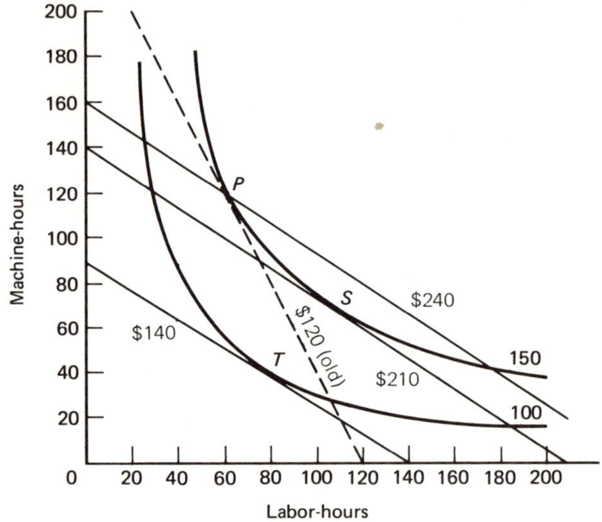

Figure 3.8 Price Changes

This substitution effect is only half the story. As we noted above, even with substitution the cost of producing each output has risen. The marginal cost per unit has risen to $1.40 per unit from the old marginal cost of $0.80. The firm will be forced to recalculate its most profitable output, using the methods discussed earlier. Let us assume that it now finds its best output to be 100 units. It will, therefore, produce at point *T*, using less machinery and less labor than at point S. This movement from S to *T* is called the *output effect* of a price change.

The complete result of a price change is the sum of the substitution effect and the output effect, that is, the movement from *P* to *T*. Since both these movements decrease the use of machinery, the total effect will certainly be a decrease in machine-hours. In this case, there is a decrease of 60 hours through the substitution effect and 20 more through the output effect, making a total decrease of 80 hours. The effect on the use of labor is less clear. The substitution effect, the movement from *P* to S, requires more labor; the output effect, the movement from S to *T*, means less labor. In this particular case, the substitution effect produced an increase of 60 labor-hours and the output effect a decrease of 40 hours, making a net increase of 20 hours. This increase is an accident of this particular case. The net effect could have been an increase, a decrease, or no change, although the last is unlikely. If the substitution effect is stronger, there will be an increase; if the output effect is stronger, there will be a decrease; only if the two exactly cancel will there be no change. The strength of the substitution effect depends mainly on the technology of production; that of the output effect depends upon the demand for the product. The facts of the situation determine their relative strengths in a particular case.

We have discussed only the effects of a price increase. The effects of a price decrease are similar. A decrease in machinery prices will increase the use of machinery, but will increase the use of labor only if the output effect dominates. If the substitution effect is stronger, the use of labor will decrease.

THE INDIVIDUAL SUPPLY CURVE

The logic of the quantity supplied by a firm has already been discussed, but it is now time to put this discussion in the form of a supply curve. The firm will wish to sell any quantity for which marginal revenue exceeds its marginal cost. We can therefore say that the marginal cost curve is the supply curve of the firm. This marginal cost curve will normally tend to rise throughout the pertinent regions.

This designation is subject to two qualifications. The first is that the marginal cost curve gives the quantity that will be supplied at a specific *marginal revenue*. Most textbooks describe the supply curve differently, as the amount that would be offered at a given *price*. If the demand curve is horizontal, price and marginal revenue are the same, so our definition agrees with the usual one. If the demand curve is sloping, the marginal revenue and the price are different. In such a case, the usual demand curve does not exist, for it is impossible to tell how much will be supplied simply by knowing the price; we need to know the marginal revenue. We have chosen this different definition, because it holds for all cases.

The second problem in using the marginal cost curve as the supply curve is to determine what portion of it makes up the supply curve. Clearly, at large outputs the firm is willing to increase production as long as there is an additional profit to be obtained from additional production. The difficulty is at the lower end of the scale. How low should a firm permit its output to fall before it shuts down? At first thought, we are tempted to say that a firm should shut down whenever it loses money. This is not correct, for a firm that shuts down also loses money; the fixed costs continue even if production does not. A firm interested in minimizing losses should shut down only if it loses more money by operating than by not operating. This means that a firm should operate as long as its loss is less than its fixed cost. If we put this statement in a slightly different way, a firm should operate if it can cover all its variable costs and have anything left over toward fixed costs. The shut-down point comes when total revenue falls below variable cost, or when average revenue falls below average variable cost. This rule corresponds with the marginal analysis that we have been using. The extra cost of operating is the variable cost; the firm should operate only when the extra revenue exceeds the extra cost, that is, if total revenue exceeds variable cost.

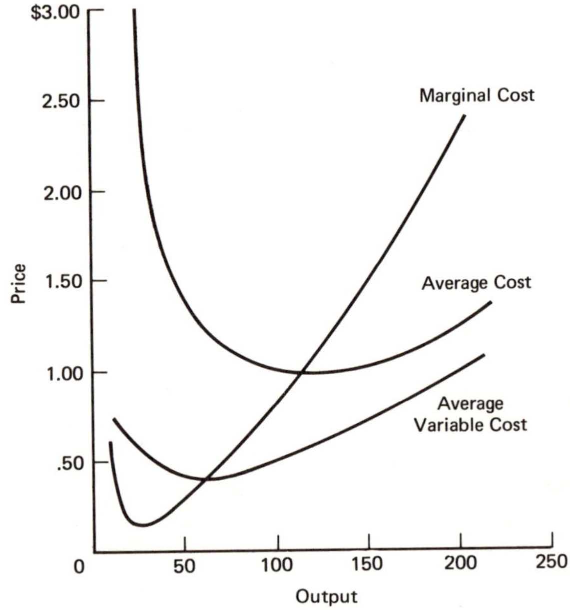

Figure 3.9 Supply Curve

We can, therefore, say that the marginal cost curve indicates the amount that will be supplied at any given marginal revenue, if the average revenue (price) at this point is greater than the average variable cost. This rule is rather complicated, because it combines marginal and average concepts. If the demand curve for the product is horizontal, the rule is simplified, for the marginal revenue and average revenue are the same. In this case, we can say that the marginal cost curve tells us what quantity will be supplied at any given price, as long as that price exceeds the average variable cost. Such a supply curve is shown in Figure 3.9; it is the upper portion of the marginal cost curve.

In referring to a supply curve, we have implicitly assumed that the firm knows its marginal cost curve. In many cases, of course, it does not, but it usually has some idea of what that cost curve would be. It can therefore come to some decision about what quantity to supply at any specified level of marginal revenue. The better the management of the firm, the more solidly based the decision will be.

4

PURE COMPETITION

We have examined the behavior of firms and households in some detail. We now will consider the markets where they come together to buy and sell products and factors of production. For ease in discussion, markets are often classified into certain types.

At one extreme is *pure competition,* with many independent firms selling identical products to many independent buyers. At the other extreme is *monopoly,* with only a single seller. In between are the industries where competition exists, but not pure competition. These intermediate cases are sometimes grouped together as *imperfect competition.* The imperfection may be that there are only a few sellers or that the products sold are not identical. We call the latter case *monopolistic competition,* for each company has a monopoly of its own particular brand or location, but competes with other similar ones. (Retail grocery stores are an example of monopolistic competition.) An industry is called an *oligopoly* if it has only a few sellers. Sometimes oligopolies are classified as *homogeneous,* if they sell identical products and *heterogeneous,* if they sell differentiated products. The plate glass industry is a homogeneous oligopoly, the automobile industry, a heterogeneous oligopoly. The heterogeneous oligopoly has the characteristics of oligopoly and monopolistic competition. It is probably the most common market type in American manufacturing.

Of all the types of markets, economists have given most attention to pure competition, although it seldom exists in real life. By definition, it excludes all brand-name products and all cases of special advantage due to location. Even agriculture, which comes closest, seldom fits the definition. In some markets, the government interferes to provide concerted action, ruling out independence. In other markets, especially for meats, fresh produce, and tobacco, the number of buyers in particular localities is small. Since pure competition is so rare, economists have been accused of talking about it only because it is easily understood, like the man who lost a half dollar on Eleventh Street but looked for it on Twelfth because the light was better. There is some truth to this criticism, since pure competition is the case for which we can give the best explanation. There are, however, two other reasons. One is that many of the principles of pure competition apply to other types of markets, and it is easier to learn them first from the simple example. The second reason is that pure competition produces "ideal" results and is, therefore, worth discussing as a model and yardstick. (We will discuss the sense in which these results are ideal at the end of this chapter.)

Just as it is useful to take up types of markets one by one, we will find it useful to analyze each type in stages. We must remember, however, that the categories we use, such as short run and long run, are created mainly for convenience. Many actual problems do not fit into any one category.

SHORT-RUN EQUILIBRIUM

If there are many independent firms selling the same product, consumers will have no preference for any one of them. Each must sell its product at the market price, for even a slight increase would cause customers to shift to its competitors. It also has no reason to sell for less, for it can sell its entire output at the market price. Even if it doubled its output, it would have a negligible effect on the total market, because it is only one of a great many firms. Its demand curve is, therefore, virtually horizontal.

We saw in Chapter 3 that, for a firm in such a position, its marginal cost curve is its supply curve. The horizontal demand curve means that the price equals the marginal revenue. The marginal cost curve, therefore, tells us how much the firm will want to sell at the market price. If the market price changes, the firm will face a new demand curve, also horizontal, but at a different level. Again, the marginal cost curve will determine the quantity supplied.

In order to discuss an industry, we need to know its total supply and demand curve. In Chapter 2, we saw that a total demand curve is obtained by adding, at each price, the quantity demanded by each household. This addition gives the entire quantity demanded in the market at each price, and these quantities form the market demand curve. In the same way, we can obtain the market supply curve by adding the quantities supplied by each firm at each price. In Figure 4.1, we have drawn the supply and demand curves for the industry and for one firm in the industry. For convenience, we have assumed that there are fifteen hundred firms, each with the same supply curve. The industry quantities are, therefore, fifteen hundred times as large as the firm.

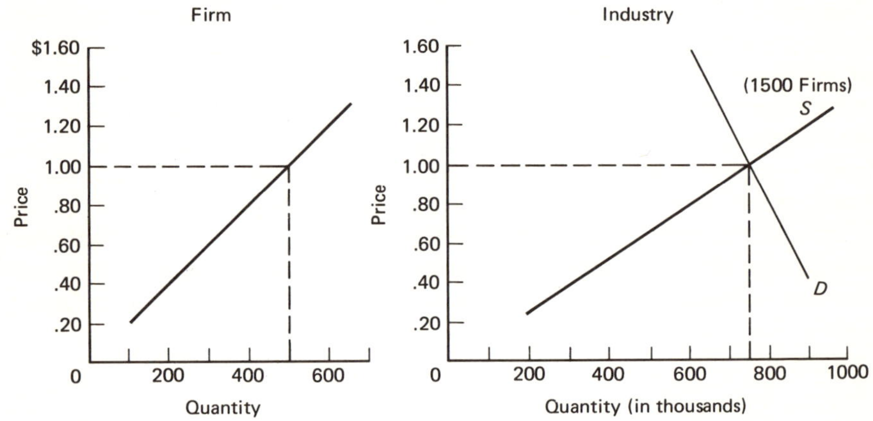

Figure 4.1 Pure Competition

Equilibrium in the industry occurs at a market price of $1.00, where the supply and demand curves cross. If the prices were above $1.00, the amount offered for sale would be greater than the amount demanded. Some sellers, unable to make any sale, would be willing to cut prices. At lower prices, more buyers appear, until finally there are no longer any unsatisfied sellers. This will occur at $1.00. At prices below $1.00, some buyers will be, or expect to be, left out. They will, therefore, tend to bid up prices, or, at least, willingly accept price increases by sellers. As prices rise, the amount demanded declines and the amount sellers will supply increases. When the price rises to $1.00, there will be no more unsatisfied buyers, so the tendency toward price increases ceases. We see, therefore, that $1.00 is the equilibrium price, from which neither buyers nor sellers will tend to move.

The forces that cause the price to rise to $1.00 illustrate two important functions performed by price increases. The rise in prices serves as an incentive to producers to increase output and also as a rationing device that forces consumers to reduce their purchases. It is significant that whenever we control prices, as in wartime, it is necessary to provide alternative mechanisms to handle the incentive and rationing functions that price normally performs.

LONG-RUN ADJUSTMENT

The explanation we have just given is satisfactory only for short-run market behavior. As we saw in Chapter 3, the short-run period permits only adjustments that can be made by the original number of firms with their original plants. In the long run, new firms may enter the industry, or old firms may change their scale of operations, that is, add to or decrease plant capacity. For the moment, let us speak as if the only long-run adjustment comes from entry of new firms into the industry or the exit of old firms, without any changes in the size of the remaining old firms. The entry of new firms clearly takes time, time for newcomers to perceive the opportunities, time for organization and financing, and time to arrange the physical operations of the new firm. The rate of entry of new firms obviously varies from time to time and from country to country. Indeed, whole theories of economic development have been based upon national differences in this response rate.

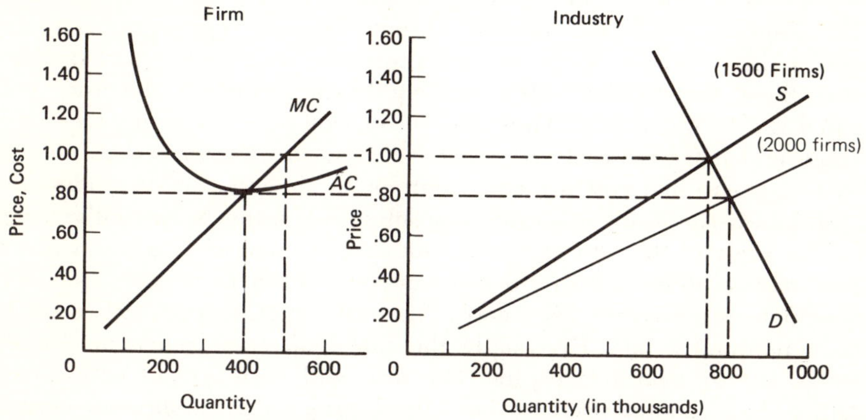

Figure 4.2 Long-Run Equilibrium—Entry

The most important signal for new firms to enter a market is that old firms are making a profit. (Remember that we defined profit as being above the return on investment and the wages of the owners. In accounting terms, the signal is high profit.) New firms, wishing to share the profit, will enter the industry, thus shifting the supply curve to the right and lowering the price. This process of entry tends to continue as long as there are profits, for the alternative to establishing a new firm is to be an employee and receive wages but no profit. The new entries ultimately eliminate all profit from the industry, and the industry returns to equilibrium, for no firm can improve its position either by entering or by leaving the industry. In Figure 4.2 we have a diagram of this long-run adjustment. We return to the industry and the single firm of Figure 4.1. The industry has reached its short-run equilibrium position at a price of $1.00, with each firm supplying 500 units. In order to discover if this is a long-run equilibrium, we have also drawn the average cost curve for the firm. With this average cost curve, the firm is making a profit of $0.18 per unit, for its average revenue is $1.00, and the average cost, for an output of 500 units, is $0.82. This profit will induce other firms to enter the industry, shifting the supply curve to the right and lowering the price. When the number of firms has risen to two thousand, we see that the price has fallen to $0.80. The total quantity supplied by the industry has increased, at this price, to 800,000 units, although each firm is supplying only 400 units, less than its original amount.

When the price has fallen to $0.80, there will be no more profit, for the marginal cost curve crosses the average cost curve at this point. There will, therefore, be no further entry of new firms into the industry. The long-run equilibrium has been established at this point, which also represents the minimum cost of production. This is not an accident of our diagram, but a necessary condition. The long-run equilibrium requires that there be no profit, and therefore price must equal *average cost.* Since this is also a short-run equilibrium position, the price will equal the *marginal cost.* These can occur simultaneously only when average and marginal cost are equal. We saw in Chapter 3 that average cost and marginal cost are equal only at the lowest cost of production.

If the existing firms in an industry suffer losses, this is, naturally, a signal for some of them to leave the industry. We saw in Chapter 3 that a firm may continue in business if it can cover its variable costs, even if it does not also cover its fixed costs. Naturally, such a condition can only be a temporary one. Eventually the time will come when machinery wears out or contracts expire. The firm will then go out of business rather than commit itself to these fixed costs for an additional period. When an item of fixed cost must be renewed or replaced, the fixed cost becomes variable, and variable costs are undertaken only when they can be covered.

It is often a cause of concern to a country when a large and important industry suffers losses over a period of time. In such cases, the government is frequently asked to intervene so as to enable firms to make normal returns (and keep their normal number of employees). Such intervention may include licenses to prevent new firms from replacing failing ones, the imposition of tariffs on competing foreign goods, the purchase of excess supply by the government, or simple direct subsidy. Such policies are designed to ease the difficulties faced by industries which produce more than customers want. From our present discussion, we can also see that these policies delay eventual adjustment.

Figure 4.3 shows the course of adjustment to lower output. We have assumed the same initial conditions of supply, but a lower demand has forced the price down to $0.60. At this level, the firm is losing $0.23 per item, but we will assume that this loss is less than the fixed cost. Eventually, however, some firms will find it profitable to drop out, as old contracts expire and old machinery wears out. As these firms leave, the supply curve shifts to the left and the price rises. When it returns to $0.80, the remaining one thousand firms are again breaking even, so the exodus stops. The industry supply decreases to 400,000 but each firm has expanded.

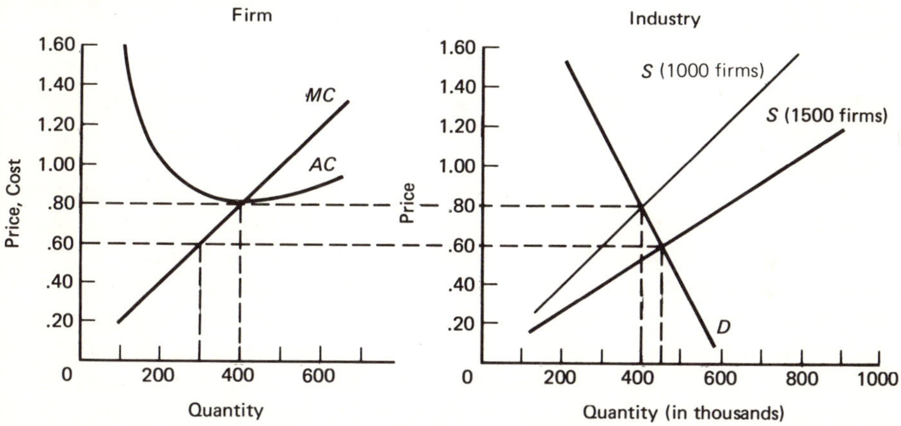

Figure 4.3 Long-Run Equilibrium—Exit

Taking Figures 4.2 and 4.3 together, we see that no matter where we start, final equilibrium occurs at a price of $0.80, which is the minimum cost of production. This result is sometimes described by saying that the long-run supply curve is horizontal. This is also what economists of the nineteenth century meant when they said that long-run price was determined by the cost of production, regardless of the demand.

INTERNAL AND EXTERNAL ECONOMIES

We must now ask to what extent these results depend on our assumptions. We assumed, for example, that each firm had exactly the same cost curve. This was merely for convenience in drawing the diagrams, since otherwise it would have been necessary to draw all the cost curves and add them, whereas we could simply multiply if they were identical. For the market to operate as in Figures 4.2 and 4.3, it is necessary only that each firm has the same minimum cost of production. If this is not the case, new firms using the cheaper method will enter the industry, prices will fall, and eventually the high cost firms will be driven out of business. Different methods of production can coexist in an industry only if they are equally efficient when each is operating at its best level. This phenomenon is not uncommon in American industries, where large and small firms often operate side by side.

Sometimes, however, we find that larger firms can produce an article more cheaply than small ones. In such a case, we say there are *economies of scale,* or, in the layman's phrase, economies of mass production. We call these *internal economies* because they depend only upon the size of the firm itself. These economies of scale occur in the area of increasing returns that we found in the production curves of Chapter 3. They are, in large part, the result of the fact that certain methods of mass production require a very large fixed plant to be usable at all. This indivisibility may make the most efficient scale quite large, at least in certain industries.

Americans are so accustomed to the economies of mass production that they often forget that there are also *internal diseconomies of scale,* which force costs up as a firm becomes larger. These reflect the operation of the law of diminishing returns. In most manufacturing, they result from the strain on the fixed factor, management, as operations become too large and varied. It is significant that much of the study of business administration is devoted to methods of communications and decision making that will enable managers to supervise vast firms. The attempt to overcome these diseconomies is responsible for operations research, the use of computing equipment to handle masses of data, and study of decentralization of decision making.

We also assumed, in our discussion of long-run adjustment, that all changes in size of an industry resulted from changes in the number of firms rather than from changes in the size of existing firms. It must be evident from this discussion that, in pure competition, each firm must rapidly achieve its most efficient size, where internal economies and diseconomies balance, or perish. There will be little scope left for internal changes in scale after this initial adjustment, so the industry does, in fact, adjust by adding or subtracting firms.

Sometimes we see an apparent exception to this rule of identical minimum cost—a firm whose balance sheet shows an accounting cost lower than that of the rest of the industry. This can usually be explained by the possession of some special asset, such as an expert manager or an excellent plant site. Such a factor would have a very high value if purchased (or sold) in a competitive market, so the opportunity cost is higher than the accounting cost. If the opportunity cost is included, the firm's total cost will be high enough to erase its excess profit. If a particular site adds fifty thousand dollars a year to a firm's revenue, then a competitor would be willing to pay exactly this fifty thousand dollar premium on rent. This extra imputed cost wipes out the apparent extra profit and makes the firm's costs identical with its competitors'.

An important restriction on our conclusions is the assumption that firms can enter or leave an industry without affecting the general level of costs. This assumption is correct only if the industry uses no specialized factors of production. As an example of the alternative, let us consider wheat farming. If the demand for wheat increases, the new short-run equilibrium will lead to higher prices and profits for wheat farmers. These profits will encourage new farmers to grow wheat. Even marginal land will be worth cultivating, and good land will carry an especial premium. The bidding of these new farmers will cause rent on wheat land to rise. This additional rent affects tenants as a direct outlay; to land-owners it is an increase in imputed costs. Ultimately, all profits will be wiped out as prices fall and costs rise. The new equilibrium price will be higher than the old. (Remember that in our previous example costs remained constant and price returned to the original level.) Such an industry is called an increasing-cost industry, and we say that it suffers from *external diseconomies of scale*. We call these diseconomies external because they depend upon conditions outside the individual firm, which result from the growth of the industry. We describe the long-run supply curve of this industry as upward sloping, in contrast to the horizontal supply curve of the previous case.

Occasionally we find examples of industries that benefit from *external economies of scale*, when the entry of new firms into an industry actually lowers the costs of firms already in existence. This usually occurs when some subsidiary activity is so small that it can show internal economies as its firms grow to optimum size. The growth of supermarkets has permitted the growth of auxiliary services that cut down costs for all supermarkets. There are now firms that build checkout counters and repair carts. Some architects specialize in the design of supermarkets, and special cash registers are available. This specialization, possible only where there is a large industry, makes possible lower costs for each firm. Such a case is described as a decreasing-cost industry, and has a downward-sloping long-run supply curve. Probably every industry, if it continues to grow, will eventually exhaust the possibilities of external economies of scale and become, at best, a constant-cost industry, but the point at which this change takes place may be beyond the probable limits of development.

ECONOMIC EFFICIENCY

We said at the beginning of this chapter that pure competition represents an ideal form of economic organization. We can now look back to see the sense in which it is ideal.

In the long run, every firm in pure competition will be producing at the lowest possible cost. This means that each product will require the least possible sacrifice of other goods. We have seen that a firm's cost really depends upon the alternative uses to which its factors could be put. Production at minimum cost, therefore, means that no more of these products are given up than absolutely necessary.

Even in the short run, pure competition produces good results because each firm operates at the point at which marginal cost equals price. In Chapter 2, we noted that each household adjusts its consumption so that its relative satisfaction from the last units of different products matches the ratio of prices of these products. If price equals marginal cost (as it does in pure competition), then the ratio of prices also represents the ratio of resources used to produce these goods. Therefore pure competition adjusts the allocation of resources (to different products) to consumers' relative preferences (for these products). We therefore say that pure competition adjusts production to consumption in a manner that makes consumers as well off as possible. We must realize, however, that this adjustment is weighted by the existing distribution of income, so that production reacts quite efficiently to even the whims of the rich while leaving the needs of the poor relatively unsatisfied. It also makes no provision for those goods, such as armies and courts, which can only be provided publicly. Nevertheless, the adjustment of production to effective consumer demand is good enough for socialists to have chosen pure competition as the model market system of the ideal socialist state, assuming certain institutional changes that would alter the distribution of income.

5

MONOPOLY

At the opposite end of the scale from pure competition is pure monopoly, which is just as rare. Some of its features, however, also characterize the intermediate types of markets, oligopoly and monopolistic competition, which are mixtures of monopoly and competition. A monopoly exists when there is only one seller of a certain product. This definition immediately requires another, for what should we call a product? For example, between World War I and World War II, the Aluminum Company of America (Alcoa) was the only producer of basic aluminum in the United States. Was it a monopoly? If we define the product narrowly as aluminum, it was, but in a broader sense it was not. There are reasonably good substitutes for aluminum in almost all its uses. It competes with steel for use in automobiles, with copper in electrical transmission, and with cast iron, stainless steel and glass for cooking utensils. In this sense, Alcoa was not a monopoly; it merely controlled one type of a broadly defined product. It has, therefore, been suggested that we consider a firm a monopoly only if it is the sole seller of a product for which there are no reasonably close substitutes. The European state monopolies of tobacco and salt are almost the only examples of this definition. The American regulated public utilities are a special kind of monopoly, which we will consider later.

The formal analysis of a monopolist's behavior is quite simple. The firm maximizes profit, that is, it produces the output whose marginal cost equals its marginal revenue. The price it sets is determined by reference to the demand curve at that point. In Figure 5.1, the firm produces seven hundred units, for at that output marginal cost and marginal revenue are equal, at about $0.25. It sets a price of $1.20. Since the average cost is only $0.90 per unit, the firm will make a profit of $0.30 per unit, or a total profit of $210.00. Since, by definition, there are no other firms in the industry, this is a complete short-run analysis of monopoly.

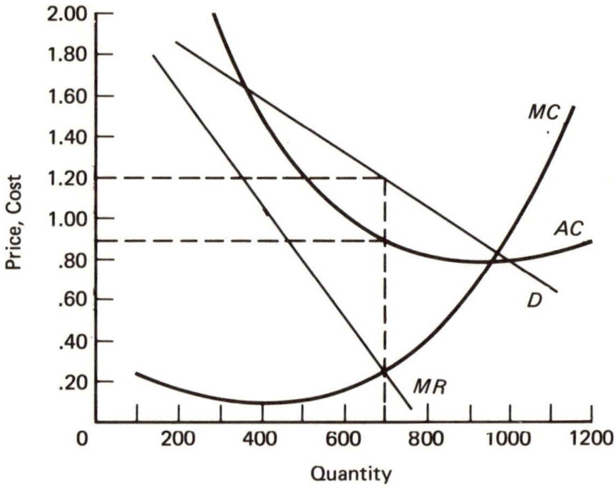

Figure 5.1 Monopoly Equilibrium

The long-run analysis is essentially the same. The only difference is that the cost curves will be slightly different (and lower), because the fixed factors can be more easily adjusted in the long run. Here, too, analysis of the firm is the complete analysis of the industry.

Figure 5.1 shows that a monopolist might produce almost any amount, depending upon the location of its demand curve, but it would operate at its lowest cost only by coincidence. No competitive pressures force it to this position. Even if it did produce at the lowest cost, its price would be above that. Monopolists are therefore usually considered inefficient because they do not necessarily minimize costs.

Although monopoly has been condemned by economists as inefficient, it is not necessarily more profitable than other firms. In Figure 5.1, the firm does make a profit, but it would not have done so if the demand were less. One example of unprofitable monopoly is the franchise to provide public transit in almost every major city in America.

MAINTENANCE OF MONOPOLY

The solution we have just given is simple, but it avoids the really interesting question of how a monopoly remains one. The profit of $210.00

that we have calculated will tempt other firms to enter the market. One can, therefore, remain a monopolist only if it is possible to bar all prospective competitors.

The simplest of all barriers is a legal right of monopoly. Unfortunately for the monopolist, legislatures ordinarily grant such rights only on condition of public regulation of rates and output. This is clearly not the way to undisturbed profits. It was formerly the practice to grant monopoly rights to certain companies in the hope that they would bring wealth to their native land. The Hudson's Bay Company and the East India Company once enjoyed such privileges. This policy has long since been discarded.

Governments still grant limited monopoly rights in the form of patents on particular devices. This monopoly is less valuable than it would seem. Part of the difficulty is that the Patent Office often grants patents that cannot be sustained in court. More important is the fact that a patent is defined in physical terms, not economic ones. Two synthetic detergents may be totally dissimilar in chemical structure, but identical in washing characteristics. In such a case, patent rights do not guarantee monopoly. In the modern world, few patents confer effective monopoly for any extended period.

Sometimes a firm can forestall competition by altering the behavior pattern shown in Figure 5.1. It may deliberately limit its profits so as not to attract undue attention. It then behaves almost like a regulated monopoly, but allows itself a somewhat higher rate of return. Justice Learned Hand, in deciding an antitrust suit against Alcoa, held that Alcoa had kept out competitors by embracing each new opportunity as it appeared.

In certain dynamic fields, a firm may retain a monopoly by continually adding new products and techniques faster that competitors can match them. Such a firm is always a monopolist, but the product being monopolized keeps changing. RCA and Dupont have managed to retain pre-eminence in their fields by maintaining very active research laboratories.

Finally, a firm may retain its monopoly by threat of punitive action against potential competitors. One firm maintained a museum of the products of defunct competitors as an object lesson for potential entrants into the industry. Other firms have been known to use less subtle weapons, from ruinous price-cutting to beating up salesmen. Often a rumor that such action is contemplated is enough to frighten off new competitors.

An English economist once observed that one of the fruits of monopoly is a peaceful life. These examples should indicate that American firms have seldom found it so. The antitrust laws have made contractual monopoly impossible and have forced firms to use other methods. These alternatives require constant vigilance on the part of the antitrust authorities.

THE REGULATED MONOPOLY

Some industries are known as "natural monopolies." These are especially the so-called octopus public utilities, whose transmission facilities are a large part of the capital investment. Gas, water, electricity, and telephone service are the common examples. Since competitive firms would require almost duplicate facilities, the cost would be much higher under competition. In order to obtain the technological benefits of monopoly without the high prices of monopoly, we have adopted the regulated monopoly. One firm is given a franchise granting exclusive rights to provide these services within a certain area, but is made subject to government regulation in order to guarantee that it will provide suitable service at reasonable rates.

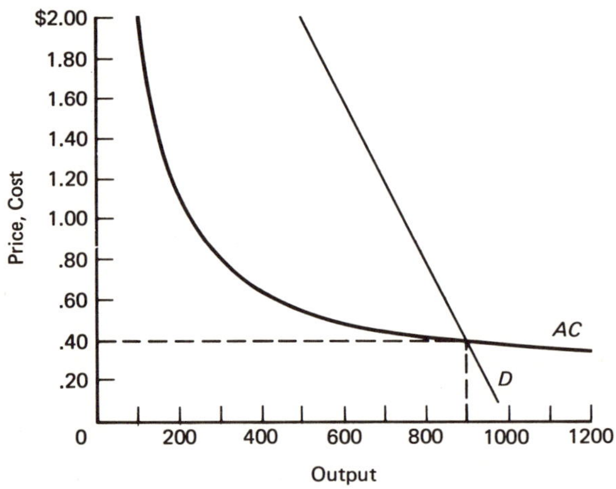

Figure 5.2 Regulated Monopoly

Rates are ordinarily set at a level that will provide "a fair return on a fair valuation" of the investment. In economic terms, such a return means that investors are entitled to a reasonable rate of interest on their investment but no pure profit. This means that price should equal average cost. This solution is shown in Figure 5.2. It is clear that the regulated rate does not maximize profit but eliminates it.

The most difficult practical problems are the proper measurement of costs and the definition of a "fair" rate of return. These problems are primarily administrative in character and are therefore of little further interest to us here.

Most regulatory bodies operate on the assumption that demand is inelastic. If this is true, rates should be raised when the company loses money, lowered when it does make a profit. In some industries, this assumption is false and has led to erroneous actions, to the detriment of the public and the companies.

One such case is electricity. It had long been assumed that the demand for electricity was quite inelastic, and experience with minor price changes confirmed that assumption. Nevertheless, the Tennessee Valley Authority, motivated by noneconomic considerations, set out to provide cheap electricity. The results showed that the demand for electricity was quite elastic for substantial price changes, and since that time many private utilities have requested permission to lower rates to take advantage of this elasticity. The result is that electricity is usually cheaper now than in 1930, despite the general increase in prices.

It is generally believed that telephone service is also quite elastic in its demand. Natural gas, which competes with coal and oil for home and industrial heating also seems to have substantial elasticity. It has sometimes been suggested that the high elasticity of demand makes regulation unnecessary. When elasticity is large, marginal revenue is close to price and the monopolist will behave almost as if he were in pure competition. Such arguments are valid to the extent that the monopolist himself understands the elasticity, and the regulatory agency can be reduced to "watchful inaction". If the monopolist thinks of his demand as inelastic, whether correctly or not, the regulatory agency will be called upon to regulate.

The failure of the assumption of inelasticity has been especially painful to the transportation industry. Railroads and municipal transit lines have suffered a decline in traffic resulting from the competition of private automobiles. Many companies have reacted by obtaining fare increases. In many instances, after the full effects of a fare increase had been felt, the company's losses were even larger than before. With increased competition, the demand curve becomes more elastic as it moves to the left.

PRICE DISCRIMINATION

One form of price policy which is available only to monopolists is price discrimination, charging different prices to different groups of buyers. Wherever there are any ways to separate groups, it will pay the monopolist to treat them differently. This would not be possible in competition, for competitors would undercut in the high priced market.

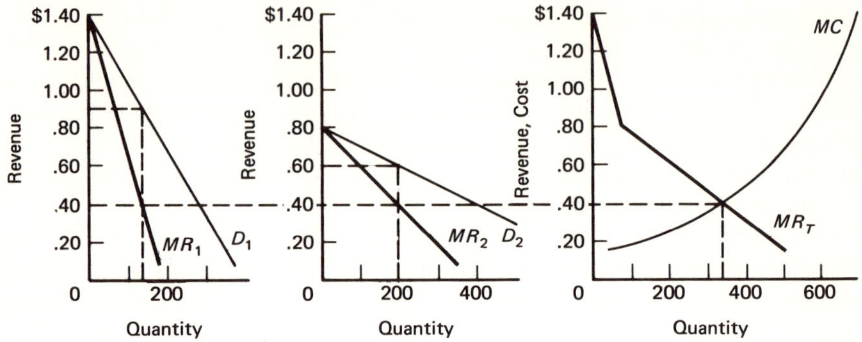

Figure 5.3 Price Determination

The behavior of a discriminating monopolist is illustrated in Figure 5.3. Let us suppose that the monopolist plans to sell his product in two markets whose demand curves are represented by D_1 and D_2, with corresponding marginal revenue curves MR_1 and MR_2. He can determine the marginal revenue he would receive from selling every total quantity by adding the two marginal revenue curves horizontally. This curve, labelled MR_T, is shown in the third part of the diagram, along with the firm's marginal cost curve. We see that the marginal cost curve intersects the total marginal revenue curve at an output of 340 units, and a marginal revenue of \$.40. When we look back at the individual markets, we see that this marginal revenue corresponds to a quantity of 140 and a price of \$.89 in the first market, and to a quantity of 200 and a price of \$.60 in the second. Thus, the firm would maximize its profits by charging \$.89 in the first market and \$.60 in the second.

If the firm were forced to combine the two markets, it would set a price of \$.66, increasing its sales in the first market and decreasing them in the second. Its total revenue would then be \$224.40, 340 units at \$.66. With price discrimination, its revenue for the same quantity is \$124.60 in the first market (140×\$.89) and \$120.00 in the second (200×\$.60), for a total of \$244.60. It has thus gained \$20.20 by price discrimination. (If the demand curves are straight lines, as in this case, the total quantity which maximizes profit is the same with or without price discrimination. If they are curved, the quantity will be different.)

The essential difference between the two demands is a difference in elasticity. The demand curve in market one shows a lower elasticity, signified by a greater difference between average and marginal revenue (see Equation (3.4), page 28). It is always in the market with the lower elasticity that the price will be the higher, as it is in this case. We saw in Chapter 3 that price and marginal revenue are related by

$$MR = p\left(1 - \frac{1}{\eta}\right)$$

$$= p\left(\frac{\eta - 1}{\eta}\right). \tag{5.1}$$

We can divide both sides by the expression in parentheses to obtain

$$P = MR\left(\frac{\eta}{\eta - 1}\right)$$

$$= MR\left(1 + \frac{1}{\eta - 1}\right). \tag{5.2}$$

Since the firm sets marginal revenue equal to marginal cost, the expression in parentheses in Equation (5.2) expresses the markup. Obviously, the smaller the elasticity, the higher the markup.

The essential problem for a discriminating monopolist is to find a way to keep the markets separated. Otherwise, shrewd middlemen would buy in the lower priced market and resell in the higher one, forcing prices back to equality. Sometimes the separation can be achieved by distance, if the shipping cost between the markets equals or exceeds the price differential. In many cases the markets are kept divided by branding and advertising. In general, wealthier consumers have less elastic demand for certain goods. In such a case, branding may be used to create the *image* of two different products, one of which appeals to the rich and the other to the poor. (Many private label appliances are made by major manufacturers and are identical with their own branded products.)

Something akin to this kind of price discrimination occurs whenever firms set markups on their products. Those items for which competition is strongest (elasticity is high) will have quite small markups. Where the firm has more monopoly power (elasticity is low), markups will be large. For example, department stores usually set low markups on budget clothing, but higher ones on designer fashions. In the infants' department, markups are usually lower on diapers and other necessities, which parents will buy, and higher on the frilly items most likely to be bought by grandmothers.

MONOPSONY

When a firm is the only buyer of a product in a market, it is called a *monopsony*. Monopsonies occur most frequently in labor markets, when a single firm is the only important employer in a locality. The textile-mill towns of New England and the coal-mining towns of Pennsylvania were cases of labor monopsony, although better transportation is widening labor markets and lessening monopsony power.

A monopsony normally faces a sloping supply curve of labor, since workers will offer different amounts of work at different wages. The monopsony may be unwilling to hire additional labor because the increased wage required would have to be paid to all workers. It will, therefore, prefer to keep employment low as a means of holding wages down.

To analyze this case, we use the term *marginal factor cost.* The marginal factor cost is the increase in total factor cost caused by hiring one more unit of the factor. Just as marginal revenue-product is the marginal *revenue* per unit of input, so marginal factor cost is the marginal *cost* per unit of input.

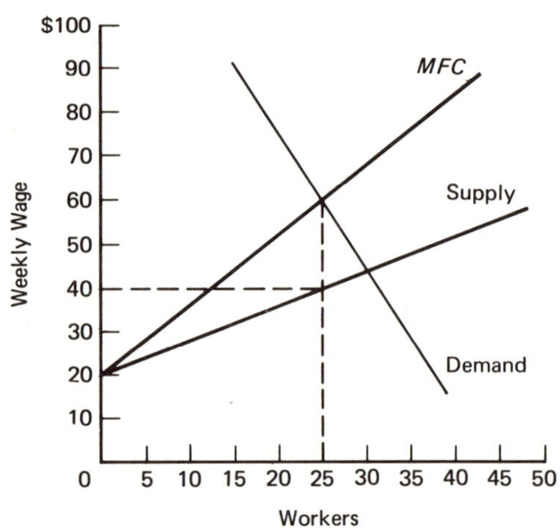

Figure 5.4 Monopsony

For a monopsony, the marginal factor cost is higher than the wage. The marginal factor cost equals the wage of the last worker to be hired, plus the increase in total wages paid to previously hired workers. In Figure 5.4, this marginal factor cost is shown, together with the demand and supply curves of labor. The firm will hire additional workers only until the marginal cost per worker crosses the marginal revenue-product, that is, where the marginal factor cost crosses the demand curve for labor. The employer will, therefore, hire twenty-five men, paying a weekly wage of $40.00. An additional man would be worth $56.00 to the firm, far more than the regular weekly wage. The extra cost of that man would be more, however, since the wage of each of the previous twenty-five workers would rise by $0.80, making the marginal factor cost more than $61.00, which is higher than the marginal revenue-product.

If an employer can discriminate among employees, he can sometimes escape this problem. Usually, this requires complete secrecy about wages. When this is possible, an additional worker can be hired without affecting the wages of previous workers. In such a case, the marginal factor cost is only the wage of the additional worker, and the employer will hire the number of workers determined by the intersection of the demand and supply curves. The firm in Figure 5.3 will hire thirty workers, and there will be no such thing as a wage rate, since every worker is differently compensated. Such hiring practices are rare for ordinary workers, since the secrecy required is impossible, but they exist for professional and executive groups.

These cases can occur only when workers are unorganized. In Chapter 7, we will consider what happens when an employer monopsony faces a union monopoly.

ECONOMIC EFFICIENCY

In Chapter 4 we noted that pure competition produces ideal results. In pure competition, available techniques are used to produce a commodity as efficiently as possible. Production is allocated strictly in proportion to consumer preferences. Monopolies produce no such efficiency. Without the pressure of new entrants, nothing forces a monopolist to produce at the most efficient output. The gap between price and marginal cost also means that there is no direct relationship between consumer preferences and costs of production. For these reasons, economists have argued that pure competition is the best type of market and monopoly the worst.

Our discussion of the maintenance of monopoly indicates that we must amend this judgment. Some firms maintain a monopoly by devising new products and new techniques of production. It is entirely possible that consumers gain more from the innovations made by these firms than they lose from inefficient production and high prices.

In a static world, pure competition is a good system; it produces efficiently and adjusts readily to changes in demand. In a dynamic society, its superiority is not so clear. The many small firms that typify pure competition are not well adapted to financing research facilities. In the United States, agriculture, a competitive industry, has seldom provided its own innovations. Outstanding new developments have come either from government laboratories or from the farm implement and fertilizer industries, both oligopolies. In the real world, pure competition has disadvantages and monopoly has advantages that are not apparent from our static models.

EFFICIENCY AND INDIFFERENCE CURVES

One way of examining the contrast in efficiency which results from pure competition and monopoly is by an extension of the indifference curves which we used in Chapter 2. Suppose that two individuals have chosen the equilibrium points *P* and *P′* shown in Figure 5.5. The first consumer has chosen 11 pounds of beef and 30 pounds of pork; the second has chosen 39 pounds of beef and 20 pounds of pork. Adding these together, we see that they are consuming 50 pounds of beef and 50 pounds of pork. The question which we might ask is whether the meat is distributed between the two in the best fashion.

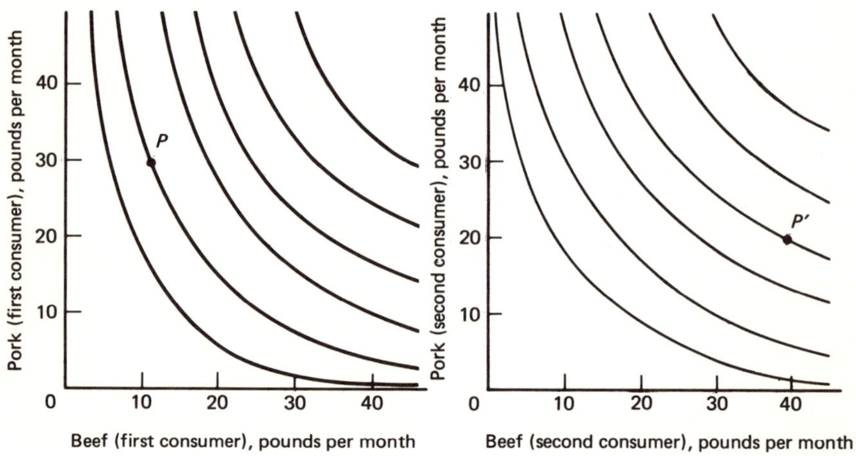

Figure 5.5 Two Consumers

In order to examine the question, we combine the two indifference maps into a single diagram, as shown in Figure 5.6. This diagram is called an Edgeworth-Bowley box, after the economists who first used it. The first consumer's indifference map is read in the usual fashion; the second map is read down and left, beginning in the upper right hand corner. Since the sides of the box represent the total amounts of the two products available, the points *P* and *P′* are now a single point, at which the first consumer has 11 pounds of beef and the second 39, while the first consumes 30 pounds of pork and the second 20.

Upon examination, we see that *P* is not the most desirable point. If the two consumers were to make an exchange of meats, it would be possible to make one or both better off than at *P*. For example, at point *Q*, the second consumer would be just as well off as he is at *P*, since he would be on the same indifference curve. The first, however, would have improved his position, for *Q* is better than *P*. At point *R*, the second consumer would have improved his position at no cost to the first. If we look at the cigar-shaped area *PQSR*, we see that every point on the boundary is better than *P* for one consumer and no worse for the other. Every point inside the cigar (such as *T*) is better for both consumers. We can therefore safely say that point *P* does not represent the best division of meat between the consumers.

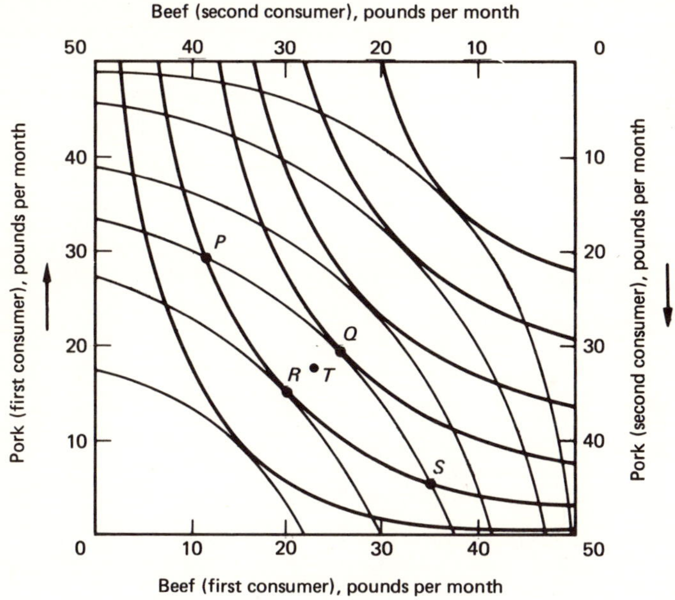

Figure 5.6 Edgeworth-Bowley Box

In a purely competitive society, the market will never reach a point like *P*. Each consumer and producer adjusts to market price ratios which are the same for all. If each has adjusted to the same set of price lines, every indifference curve will have the same slope at equilibrium. Identity of slope means that the indifference curves are tangent, as at *Q* and *R*. There is no way to move from either of these points to make one consumer better off without making the other worse off. We can say, as a matter of economics, that *Q* is better than *P*. If we try to compare *Q* with *R*, we must leave economics and enter the field of ethics.

In contrast, monopoly always produces results like *P*. That is because producers are comparing goods which they might produce in terms of their marginal revenues, while consumers compare in terms of prices. It follows that the marginal rate of substitution of producers will be different from that of consumers. When their preferences are superimposed, as in Figure 5.6, the result will be a point where the curves cross.

It is because of this kind of inefficiency that economists condemn monopoly. If the monopolist makes an unfair profit, one could use taxes to redistribute the income, but nothing will compensate for the goods which the monopolist does not produce. Only dynamic considerations can justify such losses.

6

MONOPOLISTIC COMPETITION

One of the distinctive features of the American economy is that different firms no longer sell identical products. A modern housewife does not buy detergent, but Fab or Cheer, Lux or Dove. Although these products are quite similar, there are some differences among them. Similarly, several manufacturers sell automobiles, but only one sells Fords. Sometimes the differences between products are large, sometimes slight. Sometimes the difference is only in the label on the box and in the mind of the consumer.

At the retail level, products are usually differentiated by the accompanying services rather than by their physical characteristics. Stores compete by providing better service, more convenient location, pleasanter surroundings, wider choice, easier credit, or faster delivery. All of these influence a consumer to prefer one store to another, even in the face of modest price differentials.

Such differentiation has led to a new market form that is neither pure monopoly nor pure competition. This form is called monopolistic competition, for each firm has a monopoly of its own product but must compete with similar products. The analysis of monopolistic competition, therefore, combines the analyses of the last two chapters.

The demand curve facing a firm in monopolistic competition is usually elastic, but not perfectly so. Such a firm can raise its price without losing all its customers, but it will lose some. A monopolist loses only those customers who do without the product; a pure competitor loses all his customers, for they switch to competing firms. A firm in monopolistic competition loses the customers who do without, and also some who switch to competitors. Exactly how many will switch depends upon how closely the products can be substituted. The less the substitutability, the closer the firm is to monopoly and the less the elasticity of demand. If the firm lowers prices, its sales increase, for it gains some customers who are new in the market and some who have shifted from other firms.

Since the firm faces a sloping demand curve, its short-run price policy is like that of a monopolist, that is, like Figure 5.1. The only difference is that the demand curve is usually somewhat more elastic. We will assume, for the present, that no other firm is affected enough by these price changes to retaliate. We will examine the effects of such retaliation in the next chapter.

LONG-RUN EQUILIBRIUM

If a firm makes profits in such a market, new firms that wish to share these profits will be attracted to the industry. Whatever feature is considered distinctive may be copied. If location is important, new firms will spring up in the same neighborhood. Sometimes the new firms try to provide features that are different but will appeal to the same customers (and possibly draw in a few others). Both duplicating and offsetting have been used, for example, to match the popularity of highly rated television programs. The effect of new firms in the market is to move the demand for the original product to the left. If the new firms try to duplicate the original product, the demand curve also tends to become more elastic.

The entrance of new firms will ultimately eliminate all profits from the industry. Eventually, the demand curve for each firm will be pushed to the left, to the position like that shown in Figure 6.1. If the firm produces 500 units and sells them at $1.20 each, it will just manage to cover its costs, including a return on its capital. At higher or lower outputs it loses money.

When this position is reached, there is no longer any motive for new firms to enter, and the industry is in equilibrium. Actually, the term "industry" is a somewhat vague one, for, as monopolistic competition has become more prevalent, it has become increasingly difficult to define an industry. Firm A may be in competition with firm B, and B with C, but it is quite possible that A and C do not affect each other. It then becomes difficult to decide where to draw the line. The floor covering industry includes such diverse products as a $10,000 oriental rug and a $9.95 enamel floor covering. These are two extremes of a continuous chain of substitutes.

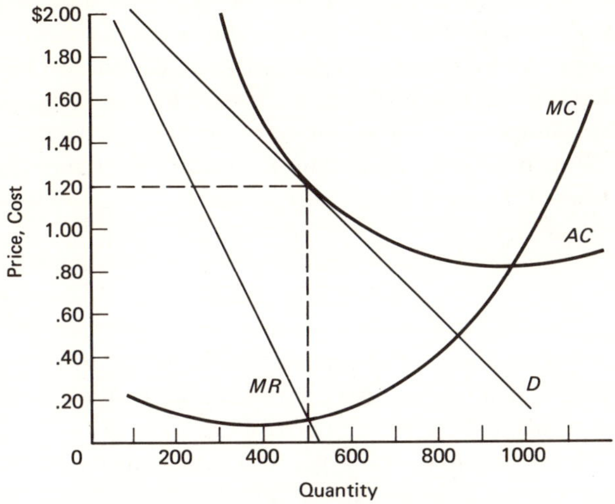

Figure 6.1 Monopolistic Competition

We might define an industry as all firms in reasonably close competition with a particular one, but the result would then depend upon the arbitrary choice of the one firm. "Industry," therefore, has become a rather vague term with a different precise meaning in every context.

THE "RED QUEEN EFFECT"

The description of long-run equilibrium that we have given here assumes a rather passive form of competition, in which the old firm sits idly by while new firms make inroads upon the market. This is a reasonably satisfactory picture of competition where location is the most important aspect of differentiation. It is not satisfactory where differentiation is based upon service, quality, or advertising. In such a case, new firms may not be able to match the special characteristics of successful firms. They may be able to match the original products, but meanwhile the original products are acquiring new attributes. Many firms must feel that the Red Queen was describing them when she told Alice, "Now, here, you see, it takes all the running you can do to keep in the same place. If you want to get somewhere else, you must run at least twice as fast as that!" [1]

[1] Lewis Carroll, *Through the Looking Glass,* Chapter 2.

Nowhere is this phenomenon more evident than in the field of technological change. In the automobile or refrigerator industry, there are only slight differences between the models put out each year by different firms. Over a decade or two, however, we see important changes in all brands. Today's low-priced car is superior even to luxury models of thirty years ago. As long as it continues to make these changes, a firm may avoid having its demand curve forced to the left and its profits eliminated by competition. The industry is always tending toward an equilibrium; but before it is reached, conditions have changed, and there is a tendency toward a new equilibrium.

ADVERTISING

It is primarily as an aspect of product differentiation that we must examine the effects of advertising in our economy. Advertising is one of the important tools that a firm may use in differentiating its product. Even where there are important physical differences, it is advertising that makes the public aware of these differences.

Controversy has long raged over the value of advertising. Some people look upon advertising as utter waste, as 2.5 percent of our national income that contributes nothing to the economy, although one economist insists that we are rich enough to afford such waste. At the other extreme are those who give advertising credit for the entire "American way of life." Somewhere between these views lies the truth.

One advantage claimed for advertising is that it supports our national communications media—newspapers, magazines, radio, and television. Although this is true, it is inadequate justification for advertising, because a large portion of the cost of these media goes for the advertising they carry. Only a small percentage of the space in a newspaper or a leading national magazine is devoted to news and editorial copy; the rest is advertising. If our communications were financed directly by consumers or through government subsidy, the cost would be about one-tenth the present cost of advertising.

Sometimes advertising is justified on the ground that it gives information. Like the argument that it supports communication, this is only a partial justification. If advertising really gave such valuable information, consumers would be willing to buy it separately on the market. A small amount of advertising is actually sold, especially certain industrial catalogues, and others could be sold. Many people would be willing to pay for a Montgomery Ward or Sears Roebuck catalogue. Nevertheless, it is clear that such cases are exceptions, and most forms of advertising could not pass the test of separate sale.

In the final analysis, the case for advertising rests upon its effect in promoting product differentiation. In many industries, it merely fragments the market without giving any firms a net advantage. When this occurs, the result is like that shown in Figure 6.1. Advertising has merely contributed to maintaining an industry that has too many firms, each too small. This result is usually even more wasteful than locational competition, for all costs are higher as a result of the advertising expenditure.

The opposite result occurs when advertising succeeds in giving one or a few firms a dominant position in the market. When this happens, the market is usually divided between a few firms, each larger than it would be without advertising. This growth can have both good and bad effects. It sometimes makes it possible to achieve a large size and take full advantage of internal economies of scale—the economies of mass production. The resulting saving in production cost may more than compensate for the increased advertising cost. Unfortunately, there is no guarantee that expansion through advertising will stop before diseconomies set in. Besides, since these increases in technological efficiency are accompanied by a decrease in competition, there is less incentive to pass the saving on to customers in lower prices. The incentive is especially lacking if the established advertising serves as a barrier to potential entry into the industry.

Probably the least emphasized, but potentially the most important, effect of advertising is its role in stimulating technological change. Any improvement that a firm can make in its products will be prominently advertised to give an impression of great superiority. Since manufacturers know this, they keep up in this race. The fact that different firms seen to be emphasizing minor differences between products at any one time should not blind us to the fact that all these products change greatly over time. Much of this change might take place without advertising, but advertising has made it imperative. The Red Queen has become jet-propelled.

ECONOMIC EFFICIENCY

Let us pause now to evaluate the efficiency of this market form. We first observe that the long-run equilibrium shown in Figure 6.1, unlike the equilibrium of pure competition, is not an optimum solution. The firm is producing at too small an output, so its costs are not at a minimum. The higher cost is the price consumers pay for preferring particular brands and particular locations. This is what economists mean when they refer to "too many filling stations." If there were fewer stations, the same amount of gasoline could be sold at a lower price. One could expect to find a decline in the number of stations, however, only if consumers stop buying brands and start buying "gasoline." The higher price of monopolistic competition is not caused by high profits for the seller; it is solely the result of the inefficiency of too small firms. When people speak of the "wastes of competition," they refer to these inefficiencies of monopolistic competition, not to pure competition.

The principal redeeming feature of monopolistic competition is that it promotes innovation. This process of innovation is usually in the public interest. Each successful change must yield higher satisfaction to the consumer. If a firm makes a change away from consumers' preferences, its profits disappear even faster than if it stood still.

Again we find that we must qualify our previous statement that pure competition is ideal. It is ideal only in producing a given product by means of given techniques. Pure competition does not contain the incentive for innovation that results from product differentiation. It is difficult to say whether the improved products that result from monopolistic competition always compensate for the loss of the efficiency of pure competition. In the case of a particular industry we might be able to judge.

Sometimes it is suggested that monopolistic competition is morally undesirable because it gives people products they should not want. Sometimes the objections are merely aesthetic rather than moral, as when people object to chrome on automobiles. As economists, we must agree that such results are possible, but outside our techniques of analysis. Furthermore, there is little evidence that any particular market form or economic system is unique in this respect. (The "oldest profession" was not invented in monopolistic competition, nor even in capitalism.)

A somewhat related question is whether advertising perverts consumer desires and makes them want what they otherwise would not. Certainly it is true that consumers will not actively demand a product until they have been told that it exists, but it is doubtful that advertising can sell products unless the consumer has a need which that product can fill. It is a cliché among advertisers that advertising can only sell a product once; repeat business depends upon designers and producers.

Even if advertising had such bad effects, what remedy would be available? Letting government control things is no better, for government officials are elected after well-advertised sales campaigns. Probably the only answer is to rely on the basic good sense and educated judgment of the consumer *ultimately* to triumph. As Lincoln said, "You can't fool all of the people all of the time."

7

OLIGOPOLY

In some markets there are only a few sellers or a few buyers. We call such a situation *oligopoly,* if there are a few sellers, and *oligopsony,* if there are a few buyers. Behavior in such markets is not easily predictable. Each individual is well aware that his profits depend upon the action of every other firm as well as his own. This interdependence makes oligopoly and oligopsony unique among market types.

Let us first examine the oligopoly. In order to determine its own policy, each firm must make some kind of guess about the behavior of its competitors. It is, therefore, impossible to give an exact description of an oligopolist's behavior. In the case of monopoly or pure competition, a knowledge of cost structures and demand characteristics is enough to predict action. In the case of oligopoly, we must also consider the psychology of the oligopolist, what assumptions he will make about his competitors. There are, quite naturally, a large number of possible courses of action, each depending upon a particular set of assumptions. Before considering the most general model of oligopoly, let us look at one that is commonly advanced.

THE KINKED DEMAND CURVE

One assumption possible to an oligopolist is that any price change he makes will be exactly matched. In such a case, the demand curve for his product is an exact miniature of the industry's demand curve. As all the firms raise or lower their prices, customers enter or leave the market, and he gets his usual share, but no customers will shift from one firm to another. Such a demand curve is shown as D_1 in Figure 7.1, along with the marginal revenue curve associated with it, MR_1.

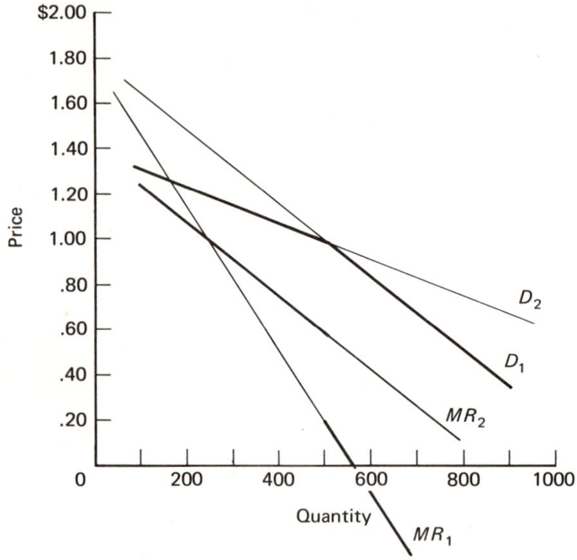

Figure 7.1 Kinked Demand Curve

An alternate assumption might be that, as he changes his price, all other firms will hold theirs fixed. His new demand curve, D_2, is much more elastic than D_1, for there are some customers shifting among firms as well as others entering and leaving the market. Associated with D_2 is a second marginal curve, MR_2.

The two demand curves naturally cross at the present price, for each demand curve assumes that the other firms will not change their prices if our firm leaves its price unchanged. The present price is shown at \$1.00 and the present output at 500 units.

It is naturally impossible to say which of these will be the correct assumption about competitors' reactions. It has been observed, however, that businessmen often believe that price cuts will be matched, but not price increases. Their reasoning is that their competitors will not permit them to cut prices and take business away, but will be perfectly willing to accept the extra customers driven away by a price increase. This means that firms expect to move down along D_1 and up along D_2, that is, their demand curves will be relatively elastic for price increases and relatively inelastic for price cuts. This new demand curve is marked in heavier lines on Figure 7.1, as are the corresponding portions of the two marginal revenue curves.

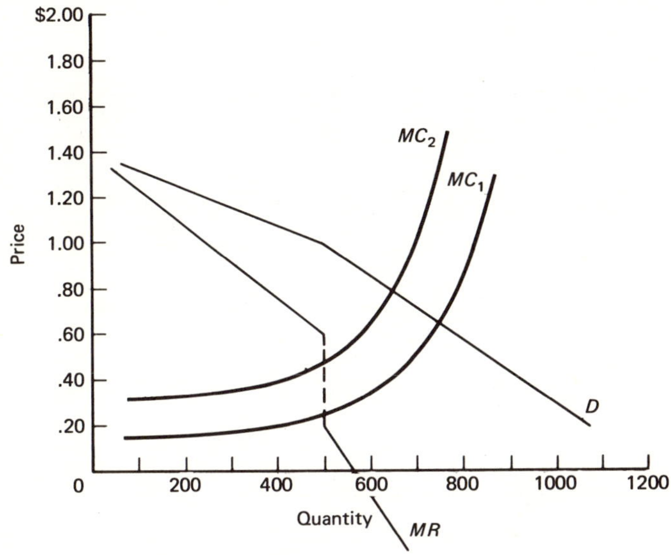

Figure 7.2 Oligopoly Price Rigidity

This kinked demand curve and its broken marginal revenue curve have been reproduced in Figure 7.2. As we can see from the diagram, this kink leads an oligopolist to adopt very conservative policies. In the diagram are two marginal cost curves, one twice as high as the other. Despite the 100 percent change in marginal cost, the firm will not change its price or output, for it is afraid of losing its customers by price increases or starting a price war by price decreases. Only if costs changed much more than this would the firm feel it worthwhile to risk one of these alternatives. Although not all industries show this behavior, many do. The most extreme example is the sulfur industry, dominated by two firms, which maintained a price of $12.00 per ton from 1928 to 1936, through the peak of a boom and the depth of a depression.

THE EFFECTS OF UNCERTAINTY

However common the kinked demand curve may be, it clearly does not typify all oligopoly behavior. To examine the full range of oligopoly practices, we need a somewhat more general theory. We can obtain this by observing that oligopoly is characterized by a special form of uncertainty. In addition to the rather general uncertainty about consumers, which all firms share, the oligopolist has a special uncertainty about his competitors' actions. Furthermore, this uncertainty is multilateral, for the outcome of each firm's actions depends upon the behavior of every other.

Price of *A* \ Price of *B*	$1.00	.90	.80	.70	.60
$1.00	11 / 34	5 / 36	0 / 33	-4 / 30	-7 / 8
.90	18 / 26	15 / 28	5 / 31	0 / 24	-4 / 6
.80	21 / 18	14 / 24	10 / 25	7 / 22	3 / 5
.70	16 / 10	13 / 17	11 / 18	8 / 20	2 / -6
.60	8 / 6	6 / 8	5 / 12	4 / 10	2 / -4

Table 7.1 Oligopolists' Profit (unit: one thousand dollars)

We can characterize this situation by drawing up a payoff table for each firm, showing its expected profit from each of its own and its competitors' actions. For simplicity, let us assume that there are only two firms, and that they limit their actions to changing prices. In such a case, we can put the payoff table for both firms on a single chart. In the accompanying table, the prices of firm *A* are listed along the left margin and the prices of firm *B* across the top. For every pair of prices, the profits which each firm expects to make is shown.

A's profits are shown in the lower, white portion of each cell, *B*'s profits in the upper, shaded portion. For example, if *A* sets a price of $0.80 and *B* a price of $0.70, *A*'s expected profit will be $7000, *B*'s profit $22,000. We have calculated this table so that the firms are not identical. In general, *B* is a more profitable firm than *A*. We have also assumed that there is some degree of product differentiation, so that it is conceivable for a firm to make some profit even if its price is higher than that of its competitor.

Various courses of action in the face of uncertainty are possible. Here we will discuss only six of the most common.

1. **Minimax** Each firm may wish to play it safe. It therefore considers the worst that can happen at each price it might set. *A*, for example,

may lose \$7000 if it charges \$1.00, or \$4000 if it charges \$0.90. At \$0.80 it is guaranteed a profit of at least \$3000, and at \$0.60 and \$0.70 a profit of at least \$2000. It will, therefore, choose \$0.80, which guarantees at least \$3000.

Similarly, *B* could calculate its worst possibilities at each price. These are, in order, \$6000, \$8000, \$12,000, \$10,000, and a loss of \$4000, ranging from highest to lowest price. *B* will also choose \$0.80, which guarantees at least \$12,000.

Actually, since each will set a price of \$0.80, *A*'s profit will be \$10,000 and *B*'s profit \$25,000.

2. **Unwarranted Assumption** Sometimes a businessman believes that his opponents' prices will remain stable although his own prices change. If *A* believes that *B* will continue to charge \$0.80, it will find it better to charge \$0.70, for that will increase its profit to \$11,000. If *B* then feels that *A*'s price will remain \$0.70, *B* too will find it worthwhile to cut to \$0.70, thereby increasing its profit from \$18,000 to \$20,000. This new position is stable, for neither finds it worthwhile to change prices further. Such behavior is rare because the businessman involved must be alert enough to maximize his profit, given his competitor's price, but naive enough not to expect reaction from his competitor.

3. **Price Rigidity** We have previously discussed the kinked demand curve, which describes a firm's expectation that its competitor will match price cuts but not price increases. This means that firm *A* in Table 7.1 expects to move up the column but down the diagonal. If *A* and *B* are both charging \$0.80, *A* will foresee profits of \$5000 at \$0.90 and 0 at \$1.00. If firm *A* cuts price, it expects a profit of \$8000 at \$0.70 and \$2000 at \$0.60. Since all of these profits are less than the \$10,000 it can make by staying at \$0.80, it will not change.

Firm *B* faces the same problem. From the \$25,000 it can make by charging \$0.80, price increases will diminish its profit to \$24,000 or \$18,000, and price cuts to \$20,000 or a loss of \$4000.

The "stickiness" we noted before is evident here. If the two firms make this assumption, they will continue to charge whatever their prices happened to be when they first came into competition. Obviously, such prices must be explained by history rather than by current conditions alone.

4. **Fusion** In an unregulated economy, the best policy for all firms is to unite. In this way, the firms can maximize their total profit and then divide it between them. With this policy the firms will do best if each sets a price of \$1.00, making a total profit of \$45,000. Such fusion

has been achieved by means of trusts and corporate mergers, and in Europe by cartels.

5. **Collusion** Firms often agree to follow parallel courses of action while maintaining separate identities. Although such agreements are illegal in the United States, they are often hard to detect. For example, let us suppose both firms have reached a price of $0.70 after a series of competitive price cuts. At this stage, the sales managers might lunch together and agree that each will raise prices to $0.90. The limit to such collusion is only the diversity of the firms in the industry. In this case, for example, *B* would rather have prices raised to $1.00, but *A* would not. Collusion occasionally fails because there is no single action that is best for all concerned. (In fusion, this is not a limitation, because part of the excess profits of the gainers is transferred to the losers.)

One of the results of our antitrust laws is that collusion is confined to very simple agreements. More elaborate conspiracies require written memoranda and a method of settling grievances, and these are too easily detected. Collusion is, therefore, usually kept on an informal basis.

6. **Aggression** Sometimes a firm engages in aggressive activity, especially price-cutting, to eliminate competition. It sets a price at which its competitor will lose money, hoping to drive him from the market. Usually this price is unprofitable to the aggressor as well, and the outcome of such a contest depends mainly upon the financial resources of the two companies, not on their true operating efficiency. Such aggression is, therefore, seldom in the public interest. It is generally held illegal under federal antitrust laws and the laws of most states. Many states have laws against selling "below cost," which are aimed at such behavior, although they often miss their target.

These six cases do not exhaust the possibilities. For example, one firm may minimax while its competitor expects a kinked demand curve. In practice, much effort is devoted to long-distance psychoanalysis of competitors, in an effort to predict their behavior. Nevertheless, extreme competition is so clearly unprofitable for everyone that stable price behavior usually develops. This is usually collusive or quasi-collusive in nature.

Although firms often agree on price, this does not mean that competition is nonexistent. It is especially in oligopolies that the extremes of nonprice competition occur. Advertising, product change, and service are all means of competition commonly used by oligopolists. The reason for such concentration upon nonprice activities is that they are impossible to measure. One firm can meet another's price exactly, and the two can agree on a collusive price. On the other hand, competitors may be unable to match a new product or a clever advertising campaign, and it is harder to come to an agreement on them. The result of this nonprice competition may be as unprofitable as price competition, but each company continually hopes that its next move will be the significant one that competitors cannot match.

Oligopoly often provides an impetus for a different use of nonprice activity. An oligopolist is severely limited in his behavior by the actions of his competitor; if he can use advertising or other means of product differentiation, he may be sufficiently differentiated to achieve independence. In such a case, his actions are less apt to cause reactions by other firms and their actions are less apt to affect him. In a sense, the firm tries to take some portion of the market and monopolize it, rather than compete for the entire market.

In oligopsony, the strategies and results are quite similar. Here, too, competition is directed away from price. Firms hiring in a labor market may compete in offering better working conditions, pensions, and fringe benefits rather than higher wages. As in oligopoly, it is possible that these other methods of competition may be more expensive than higher wages, but each employer hopes that his next idea will give him the decisive advantage. Often pensions and other fringe benefits can tie workers to a given firm. Again, the firm has chosen a narrow monopsony to the wider oligopsony.

COUNTERVAILING POWER

Pure competition and oligopoly are similar in that, in both markets, the chief limitation on the activities of a firm is fear of its competitors. This limitation obtains whether the products are differentiated or not. Only the monopolist escapes such pressure. In modern society, a new kind of force has arisen to check a firm with undue power. This check comes not from its competitors but from across the market. Monopolists and oligopolists may be restrained by the power of one or a few powerful buyers; monopsonists and oligopsonists by powerful sellers. Labor unions and agricultural marketing cooperatives have arisen as a check to monopsony power; chain stores and mail-order houses often restrict the power of manufacturing oligopolies.

The existence of such restraining or balancing force has been explained in the theory of *countervailing power*. This theory implies that when great power arises, it invites the formation of opposing power that prevents it from unrestrained exploitation, thereby producing results almost as good as those of pure competition. The full implications of the theory are still a subject for debate among economists. Although all agree that countervailing power *might* produce good results, debate centers on two points: is the growth of such power inevitable, and will it be employed to check the use of original power or merely to force the original firm to share the profits?

Let us consider the second question. This really embraces four separate situations, each slightly different: a monopolist may face a monopsony or an oligopsony, or oligopolists may face either possibility.

The case of bilateral monopoly (monopoly facing monopsony) has received the most attention from economists. It can be considered in the same way as the competition between oligopolists, that is, by enumerating the possible strategies on the part of the seller and on the part of the buyer. A monopoly and a monopsony, facing each other, may adopt almost any of the lines of action open to two competing oligopolists. Each side may choose to minimax, to play it safe. Each may assume it can follow a particular course of action without fear of retaliation, or it may assume any kind of reaction. The two sides may combine forces against others, prior suppliers or later customers. For example, the steel workers and steel companies are sometimes accused of conspiracy against the public; large food processors and retailers of ganging up on farmers. (This is the course of action most feared by critics.) Finally, there remains the possibility of aggression, whereby one party may try to break the other.

There is evidence that all of these possibilities have occurred at various times and places in the American economy. The most common behavior is probably a pattern of bargaining in which each side has a fairly clear idea of the reactions of its opponent. Much labor–management bargaining takes place in an atmosphere like that of a chess game, where moves and countermoves are planned several steps in advance. Other patterns have also appeared. Aggression manifests itself in "union-busting" by a monopsonist or in a monopolist's attempt to "break" a large customer and replace him with sales branches or many small, independent dealers.

Such patterns may or may not produce a result similar to that of pure competition. If either buyer or seller is dominant, the result will be closer to that of monopoly or monopsony. Minimax solutions often tend to lead to rigidity in policy, and the firms who employ them become progressively less efficient as conditions change. The purely collusive solution would lead to the same output as pure competition, with a separate agreement over dividing the returns.

Where one firm faces several across the market, the result tends to resemble pure monopoly or pure monopsony more than it does pure competition. The single firm tends to play its opponents against each other, threatening to withhold all sales (or purchases) from one and give them to the others. In this fashion, the single firm may win concessions from each in turn—sometimes even greater concessions than it could wring from a large number of small firms. Dealing with a few large firms, it may be able to obtain every last advantage from each.

The principal limitation on such power is the possibility that a large customer or supplier may become a competitor. Any large firm that feels itself unfairly treated may choose to provide its own source of supply or to utilize its own product. Thus, the Ford Motor Company manufactures both steel and glass, and Firestone has established its own retail outlets. This possibility of vertical integration may serve as a sufficient check upon the power of the single firm to keep it in line. However, if it is the sole supplier of labor or an essential mineral, or the sole consumer of labor in an isolated market, this check is inoperative, and it can reap the full benefits of its power.

This playing of one firm against another is done to an even greater extent, and by both sides, in the case of oligopoly against oligopsony (bilateral oligopoly). Each firm is important enough as a customer or a source of supply to exert substantial market control. If the suppliers have excess capacity, the dominant power lies with the buyers, for the threat to withdraw as a customer is apt to be very damaging. This partly explains why the automobile-tire industry, which is dominated by four manufacturers, is marked by almost continual price-cutting.

When demand for final products is great, the suppliers tend to dominate. The buyer is less willing to resist a supplier if he risks the loss of an input for whose product he can find a ready market. For this reason, countervailing power forms a very ineffective barrier to inflation.

The power of the buyers in bilateral oligopoly can be much weakened by a supplier who, by brand name and advertising, creates a strong demand for his product in the mind of the final consumer. The process of product differentiation gives the firm some freedom of action in the consumer market. In the wholesale market, however, where the firm is the buyer, product differentiation decreases its freedom of action, for it is unwilling to shift away from a brand that its customers prefer. Product differentiation provides freedom of action to sellers, and the firm, in its capacity of buyer, naturally loses this freedom to the seller on the opposite side of the market. The only way the distributor regains his strength is to establish his own brand and then contract with various firms for its manufacture. This practice is common in the tire and appliance industries, and in many lines of processed foods.

These examples indicate quite clearly that countervailing power is not one phenomenon but many. Each of its aspects must be separately evaluated. Some economists believe that countervailing monopoly power should be treated differently under our antitrust laws than original monopoly power. Although this suggestion has merit, it must be evaluated cautiously; there are many industries in which countervailing power becomes monopoly power. One example is coal mining. Coal is sold in a competitive market, but individual mines are often monopsonists in their local labor markets. If each mining town had organized a separate union, the results might have been similar to a competitive market. For various reasons, towns were not unionized separately; a single union organized the whole industry. This union controlled the labor supply of the entire industry and, therefore, the output of coal. The union was thus in a position to determine the total output of coal and to allocate production among firms by limiting working hours. The effect of unionization was to establish, in this way, a union-dominated cartel in the coal industry. Union power not only countervailed the monopsony in the labor market but also did away with the competition between coal companies in the product market.

A second example will show another of the forms and possible results of countervailing power. The growth of chain stores is often cited as an example of countervailing power that grew up to meet the challenge of the large food processors. There is some question, however, whether this power has been used to fight the processors, or merely to overwhelm certain wholesale produce markets. Is this really countervailing power, or has an oligopsony in unprocessed foods been added to the oligopoly in processed foods?

Apart from the question of effectiveness, it is not at all clear that such countervailing power is inevitable. It is hard to imagine why anyone would set out to challenge established market power when the same effort would provide a much more profitable original monopoly to exploit competitive buyers. Unions, for example, did not arise first in the industries where monopsonies existed, but where unionization would confer monopoly benefits in otherwise competitive markets, such as printing and the construction trades. Those unions that can properly be described as countervailing made their greatest gains under government sponsorship, under the Wagner Act and its predecessor, Section 7a of the National Recovery Act. Similarly, much of the growth in power in the distribution field has not been aimed at the market power of dominant manufacturers, but has been an attempt to build an independent monopoly in its own market.

We must conclude, therefore, that power across the market may occasionally limit original power, but it is very doubtful that such power is a complete or automatic substitute for competition.

ECONOMIC EFFICIENCY

Few economists have had a good word to say for oligopoly. It has all the disadvantages of monopoly and a special one of its own. When firms fear a kinked demand curve, prices have a rigidity that prevents any adjustment to changed conditions. The one possibly redeeming feature of oligopoly is that the nonprice competition it engenders may promote improvements in consumer welfare.

Countervailing power is efficient only to the degree in which its results resemble those of pure competition. Our discussion has indicated that a close resemblance is possible, but not highly probable. Again, each case must be individually evaluated.

8

THE LABOR MARKET

Factor markets work on the same principles as product markets, but each has its own unique characteristics. In this chapter we will examine the labor market, which has a number of unique characteristics. We will not discuss other markets in detail, but many of the principles involved are quite similar.

THE SUPPLY OF LABOR

The logic of the labor supply is quite similar to that of consumer demand for goods. A household chooses between leisure and income in such a way as to produce the maximum possible utility. In Figure 8.1 we have drawn an indifference map for the two goods, income and leisure. We must now add the lines that indicate the opportunities available to the worker. Clearly, one of his opportunities is to have 168 hours per week of leisure and no income. For every hour less of leisure, he can have an additional income of one hour's wage. We can, therefore, draw in opportunity lines for each wage and determine the equilibrium position for each. The higher the wage, the steeper the opportunity line. At a wage rate of $1.00, we see that a worker with this indifference map would choose 118 hours of leisure and an income of $50.00. At a wage of $2.00 he would choose 126 hours of leisure and $84.00 of income. We can plot these amounts on the bottom diagram as the demand curve for leisure.

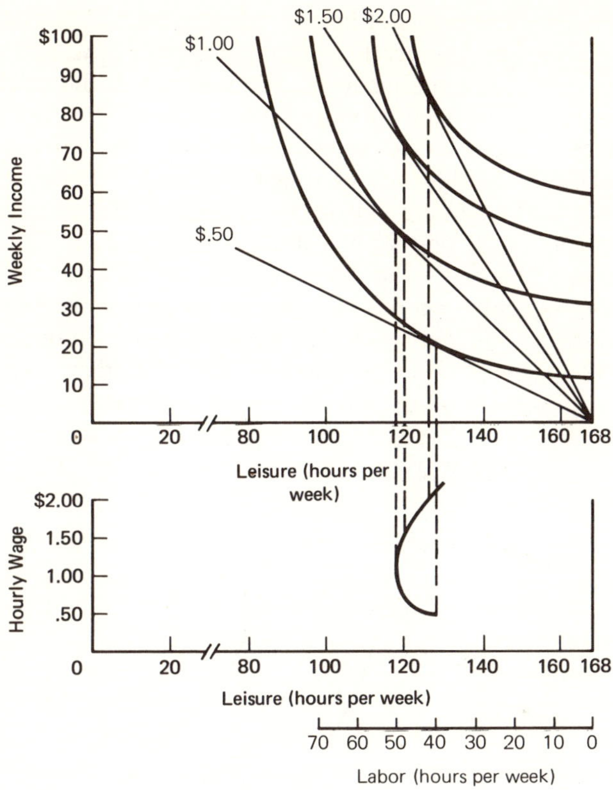

Figure 8.1 Demand for Leisure

Since leisure is, by definition, the time spent not working, it follows that the demand curve for leisure is also the supply of labor. The worker who chooses to spend 118 hours of the 168 hours in a week at leisure has also chosen to spend the remaining fifty hours working. We have, therefore, added a scale for labor, reading from right to left, on the bottom diagram. On this lower scale, the bottom diagram becomes the individual's labor supply curve. We could, if we wished, reverse the scales so that they read in the usual manner.

This supply curve of labor has the rather unusual property of bending backward, that is, less labor is supplied at high wages than at somewhat lower ones. Looking at the demand curve for leisure, we see that the worker demands more of it when the cost (in terms of lost wages) rises. We can understand this unusual phenomenon if we look at the income and substitution effects of changes in wages.

In Figure 8.2, we have drawn the opportunity lines for a worker with an additional nonlabor source of income facing a wage of $1 per hour. If the worker chooses 168 hours of leisure, his income will be only the nonlabor income. His opportunity line, therefore, goes upward at the same slope as before, but at a higher level. We see that, if the worker has no outside income, he will want to work 50 hours for $50. If he has an outside income of $22 per week, he will work only 38 hours, receiving a total income of $60. In this case he uses the extra $22 to buy himself $10 worth of goods and 12 hours of additional leisure. If his outside income is $38, he will work 32 hours for a total income of $70. The additional $16 brings him $10 worth of additional goods and 6 hours of additional leisure. At the opposite end of the scale, let us assume he has a debt on which he must pay $24 per week. He will now work 56 hours per week and have $32 to spend after paying his debt. His debt causes him to work 6 hours per week more than he would without it and reduces his living standard by $18. We see from this that higher income opportunities usually induce the worker to choose more leisure along with more income.

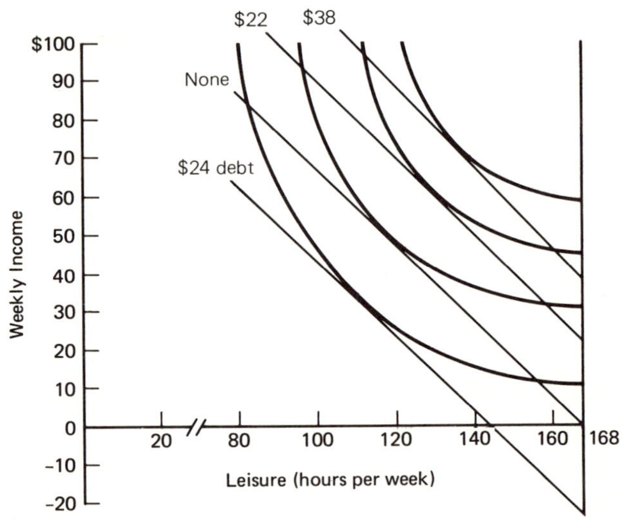

Figure 8.2 Outside Income and Labor

We would, therefore, expect the income effect of higher wages to be less work. Since wages are, in one sense, the cost of leisure, the substitution effect of higher wages leads to more work, for each additional hour of leisure costs more in lost wages. Figure 8.3 shows the income effect and the substitution effect of an increase in wages from $1.00 to $1.50 per hour. We see that the income effect, represented by the movement from *P* to *Q*, is the same as the effect of a $22 nonlabor weekly income. The substitution effect of the changed price, the movement from *Q* to *R*, shows clearly that the higher wage induces the worker to accept less leisure and more income. The total effect, the movement from *P* to *R*, indicates that the substitution effect of this wage increase is not strong enough to overcome the income effect, so we have less labor at the higher wage.

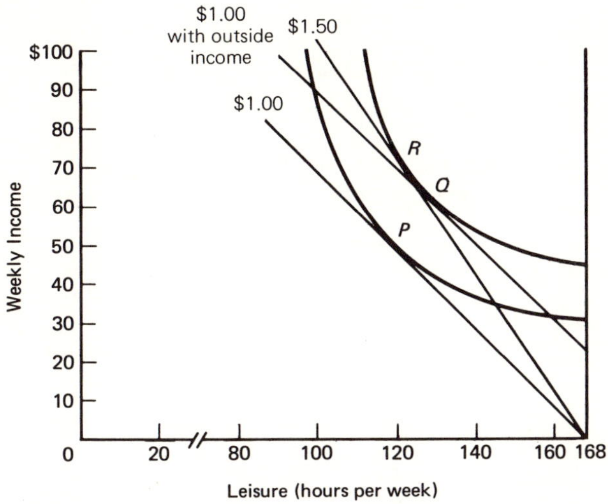

Figure 8.3 Income and Substitution Effects

We can find many examples in our society to show that workers really behave in this fashion. The most obvious evidence is a continued decline in the work week in manufacturing from almost sixty hours to less than forty. As productivity has risen, workers have chosen to accept some of their gains in shorter hours rather than in increased incomes. It is significant that this shortening of hours has occurred far more slowly in retail trade, an area of the economy where wages are generally lower.

We also observe that those who have sources of outside income are less apt to want extra work than those who do not. Those who have extra indebtedness are apt to take on supplementary jobs after working hours and on weekends. The sharecropper is a traditional example of the worker whose indebtedness forces him to work hard for very little gain.

We have spoken as if the worker can always choose exactly the number of hours he will work. This is not the case, for many firms require a certain number of hours from all workers. There are ways in which workers may sometimes vary this amount. Part-time work may often be obtained, and workers who carry two full-time jobs are not uncommon. Those who wish to work less than the standard week may resort to absenteeism. It is significant that absenteeism rises in periods when wages are high and when there are attempts to lengthen the work week.

If we take the household rather than the individual as the unit of labor supply, it is clear that there is even more flexibility. Secondary workers—wives and children—move in and out of the labor force. Earnings of the principal worker may determine whether children continue their education or go to work. Similarly, the retirement of older workers may depend upon the income of younger members of the family.

One method has been devised to take advantage of the substitution effect while avoiding the income effect of higher wages. This is the device of premium pay for overtime work. The higher pay applies only to the extra work and therefore does not have the same income effect as higher wages for all work. It is, therefore, possible to induce workers to provide more hours by overtime pay than by any straight wage, no matter how high. A similar phenomenon appeared during wartime. Wives of servicemen, who had lower incomes, were more apt to enter the labor force than wives of civilian workers.

Just as one household's demand curve for a product must be added to other demand curves to obtain a market demand curve, it is necessary to combine the individual labor supply curves to obtain the market supply. We determine the amount of labor supplied by each worker at each wage and then add. This gives us the total supplied in the market at each wage, that is, the entire supply curve of labor.

THE DEMAND FOR LABOR

To determine the demand for labor, we combine the production function with the demand for the final product. This combination will tell us the firm's demand for labor; this demand, together with the demand by other firms, can be combined with the supply of labor to tell us what amount of labor will be hired, and at what wage. Although the principle of these calculations is the one we used throughout Chapter 3—maximization of profits—the method of calculation is slightly different. As in that chapter, we will find the method slightly different where labor is the only variable factor and where there are two variable inputs.

Let us first consider the demand for labor when only labor is variable. When we were discussing the production market, we multiplied the amounts of input by their cost and found the cost at every level of output (see Figure 3.2). Now we are interested in the factor market, so we multiply the output by its average revenue or selling price, here assumed to be $2.00, and find the revenue for every level of input. The resulting curve, shown in Figure 8.4, is called a revenue-product curve, for it tells us how much revenue can be earned by a certain quantity of input, not merely the physical number of goods that can be produced.

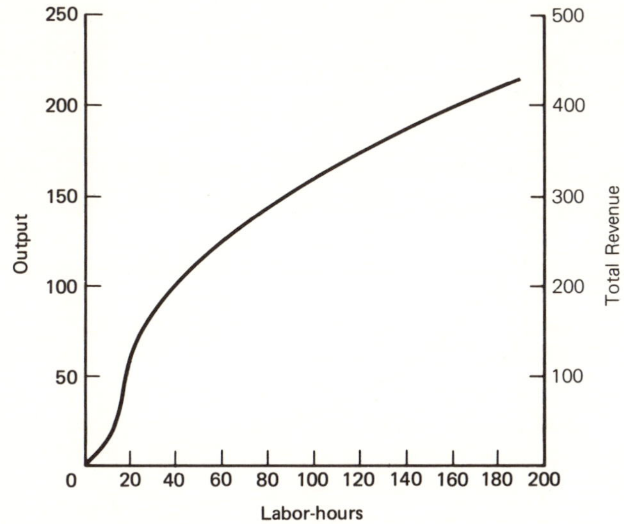

Figure 8.4 Total Revenue-Product

We saw in Chapter 3 how total curves could be converted to average and marginal curves (Figures 3.3 and 3.4). In exactly the same way we derive the average revenue-product and marginal revenue-product curves from the total revenue-product curve. The average revenue curve of Chapter 3 gave the average revenue per unit of output; the average revenue-product curve gives the average revenue per unit of input. In the same way, the marginal revenue curve gives the additional revenue from producing and selling one more unit of output; the marginal revenue-product curve gives the addition to revenue from selling the product of one more unit of input. The marginal and average revenue-product are shown in Figure 8.5.

We can find maximum profit by comparing marginal cost and marginal revenue either per unit of output or per unit of input. In Chapter 3 we used output; here we will use input, so we will need the marginal revenue-product curve we have just derived. We should obviously hire any unit of labor whose additional cost is less than the marginal revenue-product, and not hire any unit of input whose additional cost is greater. The additional cost of a unit of input is its marginal cost, and, just as we use the term "marginal revenue-product" to mean marginal revenue per unit of output, we use "marginal factor cost" to mean marginal cost per unit of input. In the special case of labor, we use the term "marginal labor cost." We therefore stop hiring labor at the point where the marginal revenue-product curve crosses the marginal labor cost.

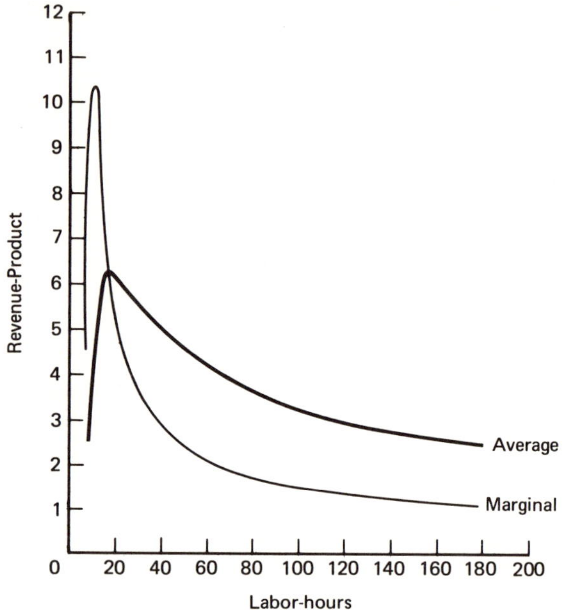

Figure 8.5 Marginal and Average Revenue-Product

We find, then, that the marginal revenue-product curve is the demand curve for labor, subject to the same restrictions that apply to using the marginal cost curve as the supply curve. First, this demand is stated in terms of marginal labor cost, not wages. The reason for this difference is the same as before: price alone is not enough to determine the firm's behavior unless the labor supply curve is horizontal. Second, the marginal revenue-product curve is the demand curve only for larger quantities. For smaller quantities, the same rule obtains, that the revenue must exceed the variable cost. If we put this in terms of revenue per unit of input, average revenue-product must exceed average labor cost, or wages. Since, in this discussion, we have assumed that labor is the only variable factor, by definition its cost must be all of variable cost.

If the firm must accept a market price for factors of production, this demand is simplified, just as the supply was in the corresponding case. The wage and the marginal labor cost are the same. The marginal revenue-product curve is then the demand curve, telling what quantity of factors will be hired at each price below the peak of the average revenue-product curve—in Figure 8.5, below $6.30. At all prices above $6.40 per unit input, the firm would choose to shut down entirely.

In drawing Figure 8.4, we assumed that the price of the product was the same ($2.00) for every level of output. If this is not the case, we must revise our calculating procedures. By using the production function, we can find the output that can be produced with any given quantity of inputs. From the demand curve or the total revenue curve, we can find the revenue that can be obtained by selling each output. Putting these two together, it is possible to find the revenue that can be obtained from any given input. This is the total revenue-product curve that we require, and from which we can derive the average and marginal curves. Although there are ways to combine these geometrically, the simplest way is to read off the appropriate figures and plot a new graph.

We can also calculate the average revenue-product and marginal revenue-product curves directly. By multiplying the average revenue per unit of product by the average product per unit of input, we obtain the average revenue-product per unit of input. Similarly, the marginal revenue-product is the marginal revenue per unit of product times the marginal product per unit of input. These are merely rules for simpler calculation; they do not involve any new principles.

If there are two variable factors of production, the derivation of the demand curve for a factor of production is more involved. It requires application of the same procedures used in determining the output and substitution effects. This procedure is illustrated in Figure 8.6 for two different prices of labor. We have drawn, in Figure 8.6(b), the isoquants of production. These isoquants assume that the two variable factors are not the only factors of production, and therefore the curves show the effects of the law of diminishing returns. Since the costs of the fixed factors are not involved in output decisions, we will ignore them and concentrate here on the two variable factors, labor and machinery. Throughout this example, we assume that the price of machinery is fixed at $1.00 per hour.

Let us consider the amount of labor that would be hired at a particular wage, say, $1.50 per hour. We can draw a complete set of equal cost lines with labor $1.50 and machinery $1.00 per hour. A few of these are shown as the solid lines in part (b). We find that the least-cost combination for producing 50 units costs $60; for producing 100 units, $100; for producing 150 units, $160; and for producing 200 units, $240. (Since machinery costs $1.00 per hour, the intersection of the equal-cost lines with the machinery axis gives the cost level.) These costs are plotted in Figure 8.6(a), and the cost curve is drawn in as the solid cost line. When we compare this cost curve with the total revenue curve, we see that the highest profit is obtained at an output of one hundred units. Returning to part (b), we see that the particular combination by which this output is achieved uses twenty-eight hours of labor. We therefore plot this twenty-eight hours opposite the wage of $1.50 in Figure 8.6(c). We have thus obtained one point on the demand curve for labor.

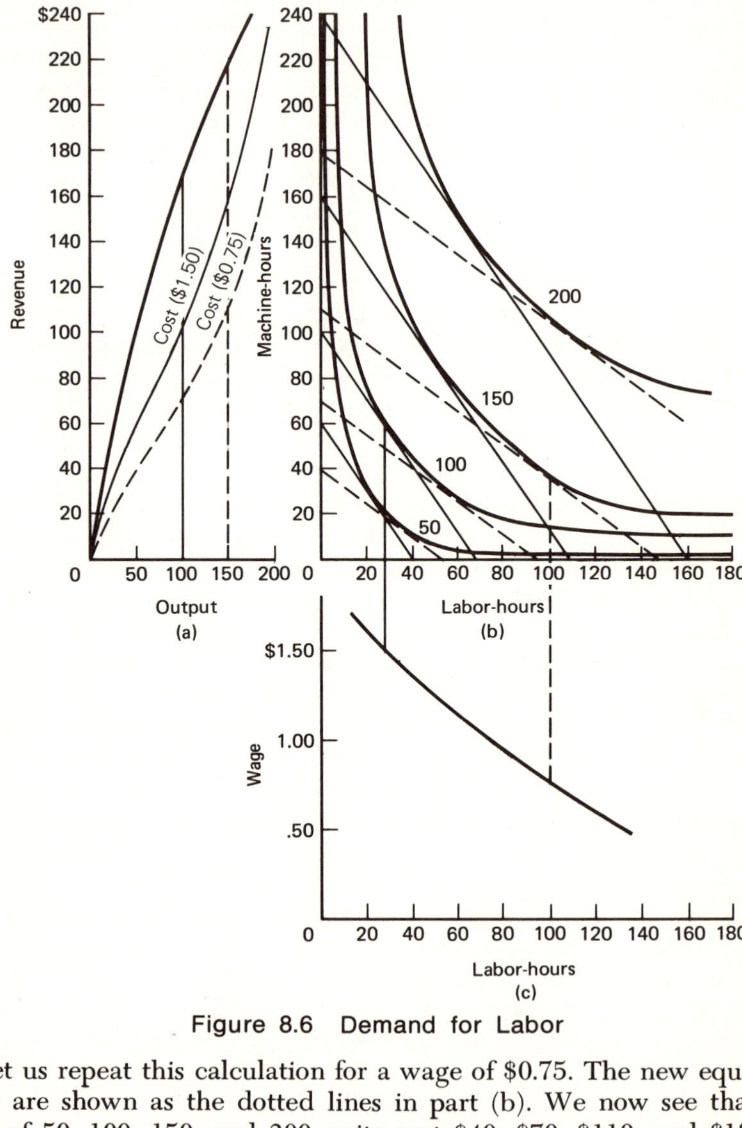

Figure 8.6 Demand for Labor

Let us repeat this calculation for a wage of $0.75. The new equal-cost lines are shown as the dotted lines in part (b). We now see that outputs of 50, 100, 150, and 200 units cost $40, $70, $110, and $180, respectively. These costs are plotted in part (a) and the new cost curve plotted as a dotted line. At these lower costs, the best output is 150 units. Returning to part (b), we find that this output requires one hundred labor-hours. When we plot one hundred labor-hours against $0.75, we obtain a second point on the demand curve for labor. This second point shows the operation of both the output and substitution effects. For further examples of the same principle, we could repeat this process using other labor prices.

We have seen, therefore, how the demand for labor is derived from the technical production function and the demand for the product. The method of calculation varies slightly, depending on whether there are two variable factors or only one, but the principles are the same.

LABOR MOBILITY

The supply and demand for labor will determine the wage in a particular market. However, labor, like other factors of production and economic products, will shift from one market to another if the wage differential exceeds the transfer costs. Care must be taken in defining the transfer costs. There are the obvious monetary costs of transportation, moving, possible loss in selling a house, and the like. In addition, there are other costs, not so easily evaluated, of leaving old friends and neighborhoods, seeking new living quarters, and learning new sets of shopping habits. Even if these costs are spread over the period of years one expects to keep the new job, their total is very high. For this reason, spatial mobility is rather low. It is confined chiefly to younger workers, whose attachments are less and who can transfer more easily.

There is, however, another kind of mobility, which is often a substitute for spatial mobility. It is possible, especially in large cities, for workers to change industries without changing location. This is one of the advantages of city life. This kind of industrial mobility tends to equalize incomes in different industries located in the same city. It obviously cannot operate in the one-industry locality. Even here, though, there is a leveling force, for firms as well as workers tend to move—the firms, of course, moving away from high-wage areas into low-wage areas. One recent example of such movement is the tendency to place factories in depressed farming areas, thereby permitting people to leave agriculture without leaving the farm.

Not even great industrial mobility can equalize wages beyond a certain point. The total remuneration that a worker receives from his job consists of money wages, plus status, plus working conditions. As long as some jobs offer higher status or better working conditions than others, money wages will tend to differ, higher wages being offered as compensation for lower status or poorer conditions. In other words, industrial mobility can equalize the total utility of jobs in different industries far more than it can equalize wages.

LABOR UNIONS

To improve their bargaining positions, workers combine to form unions. At various points in this book, we have referred to unions as monopolies. This is technically correct whenever the union is the sole bargaining agent for any group of workers, whether union members or not. A labor union is a rather special kind of monopoly, however, in many features resembling a cartel more than a true monopoly.

A union represents a large group of workers, each in different circumstances. Some would be willing to work for relatively low pay, others only at higher rates. All of them come together and agree on a single wage to be set by the union. If the union were a true monopoly, this wage would be set at some suitable rate and employers would adjust their hiring to that rate. Instead, the employer may sometimes say that he will hire no workers at that rate. Then a process of bargaining takes place until a wage is finally agreed upon. Ideally, this agreement comes about without any work stoppage, but sometimes there is a shutdown. The purpose of this work stoppage is for employer and union to convince each other that they are in earnest and prepared to make their quoted prices stick. Such a situation can come about only because the union has a certain degree of monopoly power and the employer has some degree of monopsony. If this were not true, neither side would have any hope of fixing the price.

The principal weakness of the union in this struggle, and its chief difference from true monopoly, lies in the fact that it includes the interests of many separate individuals. If the union threatens to strike for some rather high wage, some members who are willing to work for less may defect. Short of physical violence against defectors, a union can maintain a certain wage only as long as all members of the bargaining unit voluntarily refuse to work for less.

The maintenance of union funds to help support the workers during a strike is one way to preserve their solidarity during bargaining. Even so, the requirement of effective unanimity is the most important check on the monopoly power of a union.

The strength of a union is based on its control of the labor supply. This is usually achieved in one of two ways. The first method is called *exclusion,* exemplified by the *craft union.* A craft union represents all workers of a given craft, no matter where they work. Carpenters, bricklayers, and printers are usually organized in craft unions. The union maintains control of a certain skill or set of skills, usually by maintaining the only program through which a worker can learn the trade. In this fashion, the supply of labor is decreased, and the free play of the market then results in higher wages, often without further bargaining.

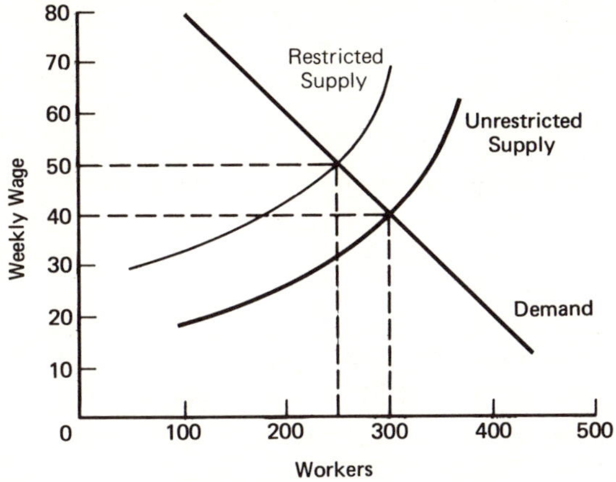

Figure 8.7 Craft Union

The wage set by a craft union is a minimum wage that the more highly skilled workers will exceed. The effect of such unions on the labor supply and on wages is shown in Figure 8.7. The organization of a union will raise wages from $40 to $50 per week, although employment declines. This is to be expected, for the union is excluding some potential workers from the craft.

The second method of control is *inclusion,* and this method is exemplified by the *industrial unions.* An industrial union represents all workers of a given industry, whatever their skill. Automobile workers and steel workers are so organized. Such unions try to enlist all workers or potential workers in a given industry as union members. Then, in case of strike, there will be no alternative supply of workers. It is, therefore, not surprising that many industrial unions have led the way in admitting women and Negroes, who would otherwise be an alternate source of labor. Craft unions usually reflect the prejudices of their members; economic necessity prevents industrial unions from doing so. An industrial union increases wages by refusing to supply any labor below the union wage. This is shown in Figure 8.8. The union has raised wages from $40 to $50, again causing a decline in employment. In this case, however, the unemployed are union members, and their existence is a real check on the ability of the union to raise wages.

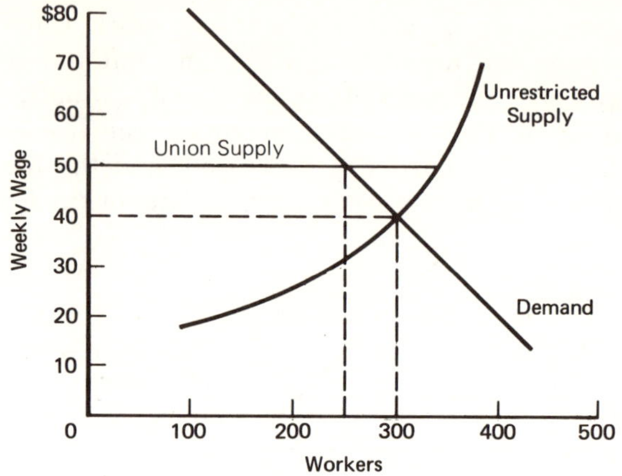

Figure 8.8 Industrial Union

These two examples depict ideal types. In many industries, craft unions have become industrial unions. Wherever collective bargaining exists, the union tends to set wages like an industrial union, as shown in Figure 8.8. Nevertheless, the craft union has an advantage, because its ability to exclude potential workers makes its activities less subject to check by unemployed members.

An additional source of strength for any single union is the support of other unions. Unions help enforce each other's demands by refusing to cross picket lines, making it difficult for a firm to operate during a strike. Unions may also contribute to each other's strike funds during a strike. This mutual support is often forthcoming, not as a matter of working-class solidarity, but because every strike is an advertisement that unions mean business, and may make other strikes unnecessary.

These few observations cover only one phase of union activity, their direct role in wage setting, and even that rather briefly. Many other aspects of unionism are important; these comments serve merely to indicate the union's function in the labor market, and indicate one limitation on the free play of supply and demand in setting wages.

9

THE GENERAL SYSTEM

Throughout this book we have been looking at individual firms and households and at the market for individual products. Such a technique is called *partial equilibrium analysis,* because it examines the society by looking at its parts. In effect, we have been studying the trees of the economic forest. Clearly this method is easier, but it does misstate the problem. In any actual case, we must examine interactions and secondary effects of any initial cause. Until we have followed these effects through, we have only a limited understanding of economic process.

Unfortunately, this is immensely difficult, especially in an economy as large as that of the United States. Some economic work has been carried out to analyze a *general equilibrium system,* which would represent purchases of all products by all consumers, the sale of all goods and purchases of all factors of production by all firms, and the interactions of these in all markets. This system contains billions of unknown quantities, and, therefore, billions of explanatory equations. It is obvious that only the most formal kinds of analysis can be made of this system.

Most economists compromise between these systems. The full general equilibrium system is too complicated to use, and partial equilibrium ignores too many facets of the system. Therefore we usually use the partial analysis and keep extending it beyond the original source until the effects seem small enough to ignore.

As an example, what would be the effect upon steel prices of an increase in wages brought about by action of the steelworkers union? We can begin by tracing this change through the isoquants of production to a new cost curve. We can then see what effect this new cost will have on prices, making allowances for the oligopolistic character of the steel market, but remembering that all of the steel firms would have experienced the same increase in cost. This is only the beginning of an answer, however. Steel is an ingredient of many other products. We therefore have to trace the changes in steel prices through the costs of steel-using industries. Eventually, we find that the prices of some of the ingredients of steel rise, and this in turn affects the steel industry. If other unions use the steelworkers' contract as a pattern, the effects of these other wage changes must also be taken into account.

The analysis of such complicated interactions is never easy. Some simplified techniques for dealing with them have been developed, such as input-output analysis, but discussion of them would lead us too far afield. (For a detailed discussion, see Chiou-shuang Yan, *An Introduction to Input-Output Economics,* Holt, Rinehart and Winston, 1969.) The important thing to remember is that the price system does take into account all of these relationships and many more. Thus the economic system itself solves many problems which economists can deal with only crudely.

This complexity of the economic system, performing its functions as a giant computer and purveyor of information, makes it a source of never-ending wonder. This compexity also explains why centrally planned economies often produce strange results and never achieve all of their goals. There are simply too many relationships to deal with simultaneously.

THE NONMARKET ECONOMY

In our own society, the problems which we face in our nonmarket sectors illuminate the problems which the market economy solves. Many goods and services produce benefits simultaneously for more than one person, and are therefore considered public goods. Among these are police protection, schools, streets, and air pollution controls. Since these items cannot be divided up and sold individually, they are purchased by governments which we all support by our taxes. In some cases, like gasoline taxes for roads, the taxes are approximately related to our use of the public goods. Usually, however, there is no direct relationship. Property taxes support police, cigarette taxes often go to public schools, and income taxes support the whole range of public services. While our average cost may approximate our average benefit, there is no direct marginal relationship between costs and benefits. We therefore are apt to demand more of particular services which we consider important to ourselves and our families, and at the same time complain about higher taxes.

Because the apparent price of public goods is zero, they are apt to be overused and undersupplied. Price is no longer performing its function of rationing the products among consumers nor providing incentive to supply the products. Without price rationing we must find various forms of political rationing. (Think of the elaborate set of parking regulations which are required for on-street parking, compared to the simple x cents per hour used for off-street parking.) It is an interesting exercise to imagine what changes in our use of public goods would result if we could adopt a system of prices and quasiprices on them. For example, imagine raising tolls on expressways during rush hours.

On the supply side, decisions are made in the political budget-making process. As a result, every change in quality or quantity of any public service requires either a major effort to change the public consensus, or an elaborate bit of bargaining whereby different representatives agree to support each other's pet projects. The result tends to be a form of rigidity in which any government program tends to continue as it is, but significant changes are apt to be relatively rare. Furthermore, all governmental units tend to have perennial budget problems, since the demand for their "free" services is virtually unlimited and their supply of tax revenues is strictly limited.

The relative ease with which we can seal and air-condition our own homes (including humidity, dust, and pollen control), and the great difficulty we experience in arranging even a slight decrease in the level of sulfur dioxide in the air of our city provide good examples of the difference between the responsiveness of the market and the rigidity of the nonmarket process. This difference does not imply that we should rely only on the market; the market itself provides *no* way to achieve the results which governmental action provides, however badly. However, the contrast should make us aware of the effectiveness with which the market performs the jobs it does.

INDEX

T

U

V

W

Y